GOLF QUIZ BOOK

Golf Quiz Book

Ian Thomson and Mansel Davies

SPHERE BOOKS LIMITED

SPHERE BOOKS LTD

Published by the Penguin Group
27 Wrights Lane, London W8 5TZ, England
Viking Penguin Inc., 40 West 23rd Street, New York, New York 10010, USA
Penguin Books Australia Ltd, Ringwood, Victoria, Australia
Penguin Books Canada Ltd, 2801 John Street, Markham, Ontario, Canada L3R 1B4
Penguin Books (NZ) Ltd, 182–190 Wairau Road, Auckland 10, New Zealand

Penguin Books Ltd, Registered Office: Harmondsworth, Middlesex, England

First published by Sphere Books Ltd 1988

Made and printed in Great Britain by
Richard Clay Ltd, Bungay, Suffolk

1 *The 1987 Ryder Cup*

1. Who was the twenty-one-year-old cup debutant who played an integral part in the European team's victory, recording three wins in his five matches?

2. Which European pairing lost the first three holes of their opening foursomes and were four down after nine holes, but, in a sensational transformation, won six of the closing nine for a two-hole victory over Larry Mize and Lanny Wadkins?

3. Who was the most successful player in the 1987 Ryder Cup, registering four victories in his five matches?

4. Which United States player lost his singles match against Howard Clark, when registering a double-bogey six at the final hole?

5. Which European player surrendered a three-hole lead in his singles match to find himself one down with two to play, but recovered to take both of the final holes for a memorable victory?

6. Which United States player sportingly agreed to a half at the final hole, so tying his singles encounter with Bernhard Langer (though both had missable putts), the half point to both sides ensuring that the European team would retain the Ryder Cup?

7. In which section of the competition did the European team gain an unprecedented four matches to nil success on the first day, to take a commanding 6–2 overnight lead?

8. Who suffered a disastrous competition for the United States, losing all his three matches, his frustration surfacing when he broke his putter during the last day singles, requiring him to use an iron to hole out for the remainder of his round?

9. Whose singles win over Curtis Strange took the European team to overall victory in the 1987 Ryder Cup?

10. What was the final score of the 1987 Ryder Cup?

2 *The 1987 British Open Championship*

1. Who won the 1987 British Open after playing every hole of his final round to par?

2. Who was the American, playing in his first British Open, who led the 1987 championship by three strokes with nine holes to play, and by one stroke with just two holes to play, but bogeyed both to finish one behind the winner?

3. Who broke the course record with a first-round 64 to lead the 1987 British Open by three strokes?

4. Who was the Australian who eagled the last hole at North Berwick to make the play-off for a final qualifying place for the 1987 British Open, and then completed the first two rounds of the championship itself in 137 to lie second, just one stroke behind the leader?

5. Who was the American who incurred a two-stroke penalty in the first round of the 1987 British Open for taking an illegal drop, but still scored 69 to remain one of the championship front runners?

6. Name the famous veteran who, in the second round of the 1987 British Open, shot a ten at the par 4 fourteenth hole, when he needed five attempts to get out of a greenside bunker?

7. Which Welshman, with a final score of 297, was the leading amateur in the 1987 British Open, despite a disappointing final round of 80?

8. Who was the second-placed Briton in the 1987 Open Championship, with a four-round total of 284 which put him in joint eighth position?

9. Who was the 1987 American Walker Cup player who, as a new professional, holed-in-one at the seventh in his final round at the 1987 Open Championship?

10. Who, in seventh position, was the highest placed former champion in the 1987 Open Championship, with a four-round total of 283?

3 *The World Matchplay Championship*

1. Which English course has always been the venue for the World Matchplay Championship?

2. Who lost successive World Matchplay finals in 1984 and 1985?

3. Who had won the World Matchplay Championship three times up to 1986, playing British opposition in the final on every occasion?

4. Who defeated Severiano Ballesteros by 7 and 6 in the second round of the 1986 World Matchplay Championship?

5. Which two players exchanged twenty-seven birdies and four eagles in a memorable second-round encounter in the 1986 World Matchplay Championship which went to thirty-eight holes?

6. Who is the only Japanese golfer to win the World Matchplay Championship?

7. How many players currently participate in the World Matchplay Championship?

8. Which Australian was beaten, in 1965 and 1967, on his two appearances in the World Matchplay final?

9. Who was the American who was beaten 9 and 8 by Severiano Ballesteros in the semi-final of the 1984 World Matchplay Championship?

10. Who, in 1975, were the last American finalists in the World Matchplay Championship?

4 *The European PGA Tour – Mixed Bag*

1. Who won the Moroccan Open in Rabat, the first event on the 1987 European Tour?

2. Who won the 1987 Ebel European Masters, going on to become the first Swedish golfer to exceed season's earnings of £100,000 on the PGA Tour?

3. Who, after starting the tournament with a course record round of 64, won the 1987 Italian Open at the sixth extra hole of a play-off with Jose Rivero?

4. Who, when winning the final Lawrence Batley International Tournament, became the only American to take a European PGA Tour event in 1987?

5. Who took the 1987 Panasonic European Open, having missed the halfway cut in thirteen of his previous twenty-one tournaments, and not having won on the tour since the 1985 Whyte and Mackay PGA Championship?

6. Who was the British golfer in the 1985 Benson and Hedges International at Fulford who, for the first time since 1982, failed to make the thirty-six hole cut in a European Tour event?

7. Who was the leader or joint leader in the first three tournaments on the 1986 European PGA Tour at the commencement of the final round, but failed to win any of them?

8. Which 1986 tournament was shared by Severiano Ballesteros and Bernhard Langer, when, in gathering darkness, they remained tied after four holes of the play-off?

9. Who became the first Japanese golfer to win a tournament on the European circuit, when he won the 1983 Panasonic European Open at Sunningdale?

10. Who had a first round of 59 in the 1985 German Open after the course had been shortened to a par of sixty-six because of flooding?

5 *Men's Amateur Golf – British Performances in Major Championships*

1. Who won the 1986 British Men's Amateur Championship, beating Geoff Birtwell by a post-war record margin of 11 and 9?

2. Who, in 1985, became the first Irishman to win the British Amateur Championship since 1960?

3. Who, in winning the 1983 British Amateur Championship, became the first Briton to beat an American in the final of the competition during a Walker Cup year?

4. Who won the British Amateur Championship five times between 1961 and 1970?

5. Who was the Scotsman who finished as joint leading individual in the 1976 World Amateur Team Championship?

6. Who, in 1978, was the last player to defend successfully the British Amateur Championship?

7. Who defeated Michael Bonallack to win the 1959 English Amateur Championship?

8. Who was the Irishman who won the British Amateur Championship in 1953, 1958 and 1960?

9. Who was beaten by Michael Bonallack in the finals of both the British and English Amateur Championships in 1965?

10. Who were the four members of Great Britain's winning team in the 1964 World Amateur Team Cup?

6 *The US PGA Tour – British Performances*

1. Who won the 1987 Tournament Players Championship at Sawgrass, Florida, at the third extra hole of a play-off with the little-known American, Jeff Sluman?

2. Which member of the 1987 European Ryder Cup team scored his first victory on the US PGA Tour, with a decisive seven-stroke margin in the Southern Open, just one week after the triumph at Muirfield Village?

3. Who had a second-round 62 in the 1981 Hawaiian Open, leading the field at halfway, before slumping to finish sixteen strokes behind the lead?

4. Who led the 1983 Southern Open for three rounds and tied with American Ronnie Black after seventy-two holes, before losing in the play-off?

5. Who won the 1984 Sea Pines Heritage Classic, scoring under 70 in all four rounds?

6. Who won the 1981 Canadian Open, his only success in many years on the US PGA Tour?

7. Who had his first US PGA Tour victory in the 1968 Greater Jacksonville Open?

8. Who had his only victory in the USA in the 1948 White Sulphur Springs Invitational?

9. Who had his best results in America in 1947, when he finished third in both the Los Angeles and Hawaiian Open Championships?

10. Who was beaten by Lee Elder in a play-off for the 1974 Monsanto Open at Pensacola?

7 The US Open Championship – Overseas Challengers

1. Who was the highest placed British golfer in both the 1986 and 1987 US Open Championships?

2. Who was the last British golfer to win the US Open Championship?

3. Who was the British golfer who finished in seventh place in the 1975 US Open Championship, just two strokes behind the winner?

4. Who lost an eighteen-hole play-off for the 1984 US Open Championship at Winged Foot?

5. Which American-based Australian won the 1981 US Open Championship with a closing round of 67, finishing three strokes ahead of George Burns and Bill Rogers?

6. Who was the forty-three-year-old who finished joint second in the 1979 US Open Championship?

7. Who was the Australian golfer, the first non-American to reach US PGA Tour earnings of $1 million, who finished second in the 1972 US Open Championship at Pebble Beach?

8. Who lost to Gary Player in an eighteen-hole play-off for the 1965 US Open Championship, the only time that the result has been decided by a play-off between two overseas golfers?

9. Who was disqualified at the 1980 US Open Championship for not being on the first tee at his official starting time?

10. Who, at Oakland Hills in 1985, scored the first albatross in the history of the US Open Championship?

8 *Mixed Bag*

1. Which tournament presents a green jacket to the winner?

2. Which tournament trophy is familiarly known as the 'Old Claret Jug'?

3. Who receives the Espirito Santo Trophy?

4. Which organization promotes the British Open Golf Championship?

5. Who is currently the secretary of the above organization?

6. Who is the controversial commissioner of the US PGA Tour?

7. Who is the executive director of the PGA European Tour?

8. Who resigned in 1986 as the executive director of the Professional Golfers' Association, based at the Belfry?

9. Who is the senior executive director of the United States Golf Association?

10. Which famous golfer is primarily associated with the birth of the US Masters?

9 *The British Open – the British Challenge*

1. Who was the British golfer who finished second to Greg
Norman in the 1986 Open Championship at Turnberry?

2. Who was the British golfer who led the 1986 Open
Championship after the first round and ended the tournament in joint third place?

3. On which course did Sandy Lyle win the 1985 British
Open?

4. Who was the club professional and qualifier who, in
the 1983 Open Championship at Royal Birkdale, completed
the first nine holes of his second round in twenty-eight
strokes for a new British Open record?

5. Who was the British golfer who tied for second place
with South Africa's Nick Price, just one stroke behind Tom
Watson, in the 1982 Open Championship at Royal Troon?

6. Who was the British golfer who shared a course record
equalling second round score of 66 with two Americans,
in the 1982 Open at Royal Troon?

7. Who was the young golfer who finished joint fifth in
the 1976 Open in his first season as a professional, in
fourth place in the 1979 championship and joint third in
1981, the highest placed Briton on each occasion?

8. Who was the British golfer who set a course record
with a second round of 65 in the 1981 Open Championship
at Royal St George's, but finished down the field in joint
nineteenth position?

9. Who was the British golfer who achieved the best result of his career when he tied for fourth place with Jack Nicklaus in the 1980 Open Championship at Muirfield?

10. Who was the British golfer who led the 1978 Open at St Andrews with nine holes to play, but slipped back to finish sixth?

10 *The US Masters – Mixed Bag*

1. Who sank a chip shot from well wide of the green to win the 1987 US Masters at the second hole of the sudden death play-off?

2. Who, at the age of forty-six years and three months, won the 1986 US Masters, his sixth victory in the tournament?

3. Who won his first major title when he won the 1984 US Masters in his twelfth year on the US PGA Tour?

4. Who were the brothers who finished equal third and equal eighteenth in the 1985 US Masters Championship?

5. Who finished fourth in his first US Masters in 1981 and has subsequently twice been a runner-up in the championship?

6. Who, in 1961, was the first overseas winner of the US Masters Championship?

7. Who was the Australian who tied for second place with Gibby Gilbert in the 1980 US Masters Championship?

8. Who was the British Amateur Champion who survived the halfway cut in the 1967 US Masters Championship, at the age of eighteen years and eleven months the youngest player to achieve this feat?

9. Who was the Australian who finished joint second in the 1972 US Masters Championship?

10. Who is the only golfer to successfully defend the US Masters Championship?

11 *The Ryder Cup – British and European Successes*

1. Who was Europe's most successful player in the 1985 Ryder Cup, with four victories in his five matches?

2. Who, in his first seven Ryder Cup singles from 1971 to 1977, beat Gene Littler, Arnold Palmer twice, Johnny Miller, Jesse Snead and Jerry McGee and tied with Lee Trevino?

3. Who beat Jack Nicklaus twice on the same day in singles matches in the 1975 Ryder Cup?

4. Who was the twenty-year-old Scottish golfer who beat Lee Trevino on the final day of the 1969 Ryder Cup?

5. Who beat 1954 US Open winner Ed Furgol by 7 and 6 over thirty-six holes in the 1957 Ryder Cup?

6. Who were the only two members of the European Ryder Cup team to win their singles matches in both 1983 and 1985?

7. Who beat the legendary Sam Snead on the last green in the 1953 Ryder Cup at Wentworth, having been five down with seven to play?

8. Who beat Open champion Densmore Shute on the last green in the 1933 Ryder Cup to ensure Great Britain's second victory in the event?

9. Who beat Walter Hagen by 10 and 8 over thirty-six holes in the 1929 Ryder Cup?

10. Who beat Herman Keiser in the final match of the 1947 Ryder Cup, so preventing a United States white-wash?

12 *The European WPGA Tour*

1. Who won the 1987 Portuguese Ladies Open, becoming the first British player to successfully defend a WPGA title?

2. Who, in 1987, finished in the first five in thirteen WPGA Tour Tournaments, leading the Order of Merit and becoming the first to win seasonal prize money in excess of £50,000?

3. Who had three victories on the 1987 WPGA Tour, a record for a rookie professional, and ended the season in fifth place on the Order of Merit?

4. Who won the 1986 Belgian Ladies Open at Royal Waterloo by nine strokes, with a seventeen under par total of 275, a new WPGA record?

5. Who had a record nine under par first round of 63 in the 1986 Greater Manchester Open, and went on to win the tournament with a WPGA record twenty under par aggregate of 268?

6. Who, during 1986, became the first player to exceed £100,000 in career prize money on the WPGA Tour?

7. Who was the Australian golfer who won a Mercedes car for a hole-in-one in the 1985 German Ladies Open Championship?

8. Who, in 1986, became the first British player for eight years to win the British Ladies Open Golf Championship?

9. Who is the American golfer who has played regularly on the European WPGA Tour since 1984, and led the 1986 British Ladies Open Championship at the start of the final round?

10. Who was the American golfer who, in 1980 and 1981, won the British Ladies Open Championship in successive years?

13 *The US PGA Championship – Mixed Bag*

1. Who holed from a bunker for a birdie on the final green to win the 1986 US PGA Championship?

2. Who won the 1980 US PGA Championship by seven strokes, beating the previous record winning margin for the tournament of four strokes, which he himself had shared with Al Geiberger?

3. Which current golfer won his second US PGA Championship thirteen years after his first victory?

4. Which winner of all the other majors never won a US PGA Championship, but finished joint second in 1964, 1968 and 1970?

5. Who had his best results in the US PGA Championship when he came second in 1958, 1965 and 1971?

6. Who won his second US PGA title at the age of forty-four, ten years after his first success?

7. Who won the 1977 US PGA title in the first sudden death play-off to decide a major championship?

8. Who won his only major titles when he captured the 1970 and 1976 US PGA Championships?

9. Who made up a seven-stroke deficit in the final round of the 1978 US PGA Championship before winning his only major title in a play-off?

10. Who, in 1978, had his best opportunity to win the US PGA Championship when he commenced the final round with a five-stroke lead, but scored 73, and was beaten in a three-man play-off?

14 *The Open Championship – Last-round Spectaculars*

1. Which former champion had a last round of 64 in the 1986 Open at Turnberry to finish joint sixth, after barely qualifying for the last thirty-six holes with a halfway score of 151?

2. Who was the Australian who finished fourth in the 1983 Open at Royal Birkdale, his last round of 64 being the lowest of the championship?

3. Who won his second Open title after two successive rounds of 65 at Turnberry in 1977, to edge out Jack Nicklaus in a memorable 'head-to-head'?

4. Who won his only Open with a last round of 66 at Royal Birkdale in 1976?

5. Who finished with a 68 at Muirfield in 1959 to win his first Open title, after starting the last round four strokes behind the leaders?

6. Who became famous for his last round charges after finishing the 1972 Open at Muirfield, with a 66 for second place, and the 1973 Open at Royal Troon, with a 65 for fourth position?

7. Who was the well-known British golfer who, with a final round of 66 in 1969, equalled his best Open Championship finishing position of eighth?

8. Who was the British Ryder Cup golfer who had a last round 66 to finish joint third in the 1960 Open at St Andrews?

9. Who, recording a lower score in each round, finished with a 68, the best in the championship, to comfortably win the 1953 Open at Carnoustie?

10. Who, in 1950 at Royal Troon, finished with a round of 68, to be only the second winner of the Open Championships to break 70 in the final round?

15 *The European PGA Tour – Mixed Bag*

1. Who, in his first tournament after the 1987 Open Championship, missed his first thirty-six hole cut of the season when he was placed fifteen strokes behind at the halfway stage of the Dutch Open Championship?

2. Who won the 1987 Dutch Open Championship, his first tournament success for three years?

3. Who won the 1987 Irish Open Championship at Portmarnock by ten strokes, with a nineteen under par total of 269?

4. Who was the first golfer to win £1 million on the European PGA Tour?

5. Which overseas golfer won three events on the 1987 European PGA Tour, subsequently finishing in second place on the Order of Merit?

6. Who broke the Sunningdale course record with a first round 62, which included just twenty-nine strokes for the inward nine holes, in the 1986 Panasonic European Open?

7. Who was the leading British professional who took a sixteen at one hole in the 1986 French Open Championship, which included six putts and eight penalty strokes for repeatedly hitting a moving ball?

8. Who was the leading British professional who scored 111 for a round in the 1978 Italian Open, when he played the last five holes with one hand because of injury?

9. Who lost the 1985 Madrid Open in a play-off to finish runner-up in the tournament for the fifth time?

10. Who was disqualified from the 1986 Madrid Open, after his British playing partners reported that he had repeatedly replaced his ball in the wrong position during the second round?

16 *The US PGA Tour – Mixed Bag*

1. Who was the unknown American golfer who, in a first-round 65 in the 1987 Buick Open at Grand Blanc, Michigan, equalled the US PGA record of eight consecutive birdies?

2. Who won the 1987 Buick Open by seven strokes, with a twenty-six under par total of 262, having previously never finished better than ninth in three years on the US PGA Tour?

3. Who won the Canadian Open Championship in 1987 for the second time in three years?

4. Who was the European golfer who was penalized two strokes, along with Raymond Floyd, for practising on the course during the 1987 Tournament Players Championship at Sawgrass, play having been suspended because of rain?

5. Who was disqualified after finishing joint second in the 1987 San Diego Open, when television viewers pointed out that he had used a towel to cover muddy ground as he knelt to play a low shot out of some bushes?

6. Who retained the Hawaiian Open Championship in 1987?

7. Who was the forty-five-year-old who beat Severiano Ballesteros in a play-off for the 1987 Westchester Classic?

8. Who won the Byron Nelson Classic three years in a row from 1978 to 1980?

9. Which US PGA tournament reverted to matchplay in 1984, and was won by Jim Thorpe in both 1985 and 1986?

10. Who won the 1986 Panasonic Las Vegas Invitational, the first tournament on the US PGA Tour to offer more than $200,000 prize money to the winner?

17 *The US LPGA Tour*

1. Who, with a final round of 63, won the 1986 Ladies World Championship of Golf?

2. Who won the 1986 US Ladies Open Championship in a play-off, her first victory as a professional?

3. Who had five wins on the 1986 US LPGA Tour and finished second in another six tournaments?

4. Who, in 1985, became the first golfer to win over $400,000 in one season on the US LPGA Tour?

5. Who, in 1981, won a tightly contested race to become the first golfer to reach $1 million career earnings on the US LPGA Tour?

6. Who won six tournaments on the US LPGA Tour in 1976, leading the money winners with over $150,000 for the season, almost double the previous record?

7. Who was the unexpected winner of the 1985 US Ladies Open Championship, her only victory to date on the US LPGA Tour?

8. Who, in 1983, was the last overseas player to win the US Ladies Open Championship prior to 1987?

9. Who turned professional at thirty years of age and passed $2 million career earnings on the US LPGA Tour during 1986?

10. Who, in 1967, became the only amateur golfer to win the US Ladies Open Championship?

18 *The World Cup*

1. Which Briton won the Individual Title at the 1985 World Cup?

2. Who led the 1987 World Cup in Hawaii at the end of each round to take the Individual Title by a clear five-stroke margin?

3. Who were America's two representatives in the 1984 World Cup, who disappointingly finished equal twelfth, but retained their places for the 1985 competition and improved to third?

4. Who, in 1980, became the first British golfer to win the Individual Title in the World Cup?

5. Who was the nineteen-year-old who helped his country to win the 1976 World Cup?

6. Who, in 1987, holed a putt at the second extra hole to gain a first team victory for his country, though his individual score was 12 over par?

7. Which country won four of the nine World Cup competitions played between 1975 and 1984?

8. Who won the Individual Title for the first time in the 1965 World Cup, and had similar success in the 1977 competition?

9. Which country was the unexpected runner-up in the 1977 World Cup in Manila?

10. Which British country finished runner-up in consecutive World Cup competitions in 1979 and 1980?

19 *The US Open Championship – Mixed Bag*

1. Who, with a final round of 68, won the 1987 US Open for his first major championship success?

2. Who finished runner-up in the US Open in 1987, one stroke behind the winner, having been the leader or joint leader at the end of the third round for the second time in five years, on both occasions?

3. Who won the 1986 US Open at the age of forty-three years and nine months, to become the oldest winner of the championship for sixty-six years?

4. Who finished joint second in the 1985 US Open Championship, just one stroke behind the winner, after being penalized two strokes in the first round for waiting more than ten seconds for his ball to drop into the hole, thus breaching the rules of competition?

5. Who won an eighteen-hole play-off by eight strokes to take the 1984 US Open Championship at Winged Foot?

6. Who, in 1985, won his second US Open Championship, only his third victory overall on the US PGA Tour?

7. Who won the 1975 US Open Championship by two strokes after an eighteen-hole play-off?

8. Who lost play-off matches for the US Open Championship in both 1962 and 1963?

9. Who won the aforementioned 1962 US Open in the play-off, but was beaten by Lee Trevino in similar circumstances in the 1971 Championship at Merion?

10. Who was the defending champion who lost a play-off to Dick Mayer for the 1957 US Open Championship?

20 Ladies' Amateur Golf – British Performances

1. Who made her Curtis Cup debut in 1986, winning all her four matches for Great Britain at Prairie Dunes, Kansas?

2. Who, in 1986 at the age of fifty, became the oldest golfer to have played for either side in the Curtis Cup?

3. Who, in 1986, represented Great Britain and Ireland in the Curtis Cup for the ninth consecutive time?

4. Who was the nineteen-year-old, now a leading professional, who won the inaugural English Ladies Amateur Strokeplay Championship in 1984?

5. Who was the French player who won the British Ladies Amateur Championship three times between 1963 and 1968?

6. Who was the British amateur who won the 1984 Ladies European Championship at the Belfry?

7. Who, at the age of forty-three, won the English Ladies Amateur Closed Championship for the first time in 1986?

8. Who was the nineteen-year-old who, in 1985, won both the English Ladies Closed Amateur Matchplay and Strokeplay titles?

9. Who was the golfer who represented Cambridge in the 1986 Varsity Match, the first woman to take part in the series?

10. Who was the famous golfer who won the English Ladies Closed Amateur Championship for five consecutive years between 1920 and 1924, and the British Open Amateur Championship four times between 1922 and 1929?

21 *The Courses*

1. At which venue is the Brabazon Course?

2. Which course has a hole of 577 yards, the longest in British championship golf?

3. On which course are Swilcan Burn and the Valley of Sin?

4. Where is the oldest golf course in England?

5. On which course are there holes called Jockie's Burn, Barry Burn, South America and Spectacles?

6. Where are the King's and Queen's Courses?

7. Which championship course is now the private club of the Honourable Company of Edinburgh Golfers?

8. Which famous hole is the shortest on any British championship course?

9. Which championship course's last five holes, all at least 400 yards long, are called Field, Lake, Dun, Royal and Stand?

10. Which British championship course has a par of seventy-three, thirty-five for the front nine holes and thirty-eight for the back nine?

22 The Open Championship – The American Challenge

1. Who won his only Open Championship on English soil in 1983?

2. Who is the American, still seeking his first Open Championship victory, who finished joint second in 1978 at St Andrews, joint second again in 1979 at Royal Lytham, and third in 1980 at Muirfield?

3. Who was twenty-nine strokes behind the winner in the 1962 Open but, between 1963 and 1980, only once finished outside the first six?

4. Who was the leading American golfer who had his best chance to win the Open Championship in 1968 at Carnoustie, when four strokes clear at halfway and two strokes ahead at the start of the final round, until a 78 relegated him to fourth place?

5. Who, after pre-qualifying for the 1970 Open, missed a short putt on the final green for outright victory and lost the resultant play-off by one stroke?

6. Who was the American who won a post-war Open Championship by six strokes and had a thirteen stroke margin over third place?

7. Who played an 'air shot' during his third round at Royal Birkdale in 1983, when attempting a tap in, and finished joint second, one stroke behind the winner?

8. Who led the 1973 Open at Royal Troon at the end of each round for his only major championship win?

9. Who was the American who had a remarkable third round in 1966, at Muirfield, when he took forty strokes for the front nine, but came back in thirty to lead the championship before a final round of 76 relegated him to joint fourth?

10. Who was the American who won the 1933 Open at St Andrews in a play-off, after four identical round scores of 73?

23 *The South African Tour*

1. Who won the Safmarine South African Masters in Cape Town in December 1985 by four strokes, having been seven behind David Frost after seven holes of the final round?

2. Who was the Liverpool-born golfer who won the 1985 South African PGA Championship?

3. Who was the South African who, having lost his US PGA Tour card, returned home and won the 1985 South African Open Championship?

4. Who was the young Englishman who won the 1985 Charity Classic in Johannesburg, his first tournament on the South African circuit, and only the second victory of his professional career?

5. Who was the young American who had his first win as a professional in the 1983 South African PGA Championship?

6. Who was the English golfer who, in 1970, brought Gary Player's five-year run of success to an end by winning the South African Open Championship?

7. Who was the Zimbabwe-born golfer who had his first win as a professional in the 1984 South African Open Championship?

8. Who was the American who won the 1983 South African Open Championship?

9. Which great South African won his first South African Open Championship in 1935 as a seventeen-year-old amateur?

10. Who won the 1987 South African Open in a play-off with Fulton Allem for his first success in this championship after ten years as a professional?

24 *The Ryder Cup – Youngest and Oldest Competitors and Firsts*

1. Who was the youngest player in either team in both the 1983 and 1985 Ryder Cup competitions?

2. Who was the former leading amateur who was the youngest player in the United States Team in the 1985 Ryder Cup?

3. Who was the other Spaniard who made his debut along with Severiano Ballesteros in the first European Ryder Cup Team?

4. When did golfers from the Continent first play in the Ryder Cup?

5. Who was the only debutant in the successful 1985 European Ryder Cup Team?

6. Who, aged forty-three, made his Ryder Cup debut as a member of the 1983 European Team?

7. Who played for Great Britain and Ireland in the 1977 Ryder Cup at the age of twenty years and two months, the youngest player to have featured in the event, and won all his three matches?

8. Who first represented the United States in the 1965 Ryder Cup and made a second appearance in 1977 shortly before his forty-eighth birthday, becoming the oldest-ever US player in the competition?

9. Who, in 1973, was the British player who scored the first hole-in-one in the Ryder Cup?

10. Which course hosted the first tied Ryder Cup match in 1969?

25 *Mixed Bag*

1. Who, in 1987, became the first British golfer to win the Hong Kong Open Championship?

2. Who was the American who won the 1984 Nissan Cup World Championship of Golf, at that time the richest tournament ever held in Japan?

3. Who was the European golfer who won the Japanese Open Championship in both 1977 and 1978?

4. Who is the Australian who has won more than twenty tournaments in Japan since 1977?

5. Who was the Australian who won the Hong Kong Open Championship in both 1979 and 1983?

6. Which famous player designed China's first eighteen-hole golf course, which opened in 1984?

7. Who designed his first English golf course at St Mellion, Cornwall?

8. Which European golf course is particularly associated with Henry Cotton?

9. Which club, formed in 1899, had employed only two professionals – Harry Vardon and Dai Rees – up to the end of 1983?

10. Who was the former Australian professional who employed the young Tony Jacklin as his assistant at Potters Bar?

26 *The European PGA Tour – British Success*

1. Who won the 1987 Scottish Open by seven strokes, going into the open championship at Muirfield with three victories and three second places after just three months on the European Tour?

2. Who, in the space of fifteen days in May 1983, won three successive tournaments on the European Tour, the French Open, the Martini International and the Car Care Plan Tournament?

3. Who, aged thirty-eight, had his first win on the European Tour in the 1978 Tournament Players Championship at Foxhills?

4. Who, in consecutive tournaments in 1958, won the Spanish, Italian and Portuguese Open Championships?

5. Which Scottish golfer, in 1974 and 1975, became the first player to win the Dunlop Masters Tournament in successive years?

6. Who was the English golfer who had his first win as a professional in the 1985 Tunisian Open?

7. Who won the 1985 Benson and Hedges International at Fulford with a last round of 64, having the previous week lost a play-off for the Glasgow Open?

8. Who achieved the first hole-in-one seen live on British television in the final round of the 1967 Dunlop Masters at Royal St Georges, Sandwich?

9. Who led the Order of Merit, winning the Vardon Trophy on the European Tour for four years in succession from 1971 to 1974?

10. Who won the Dutch Open in 1983 for his first success on the European Tour since his initial victory in the 1978 Irish Open?

27 The US PGA Tour – Mixed Bag

1. Who was the little-known golfer who won the Phoenix Open, the Las Vegas Invitational, and the Greater Hartford Open during the first six weeks of the US PGA Tour in 1987?

2. Who, in his first year on the US PGA Tour, won the 1987 Colonial National Invitation Tournament at Fort Worth, finishing with a twelve under par total of 128 for the final thirty-six holes?

3. Who, although finishing down the field, won a $1 million prize for a hole-in-one at the 1987 Hertz Bay Hill Classic in Orlando, Florida?

4. Who, with a single stroke victory in the 1983 Hawaiian Open, became the first Japanese golfer to win an event on the US PGA Tour?

5. Who completed a round in fifty-nine strokes at the 1977 Memphis Classic, a US PGA tournament record?

6. Who, with a seventy-two-hole total of 260, which included a second round of 61, retained the Phoenix Open Title in 1975, by a margin of fourteen strokes?

7. Who won the 1965 Greater Greensboro Open at the age of fifty-two years and ten months?

8. Who, in 1987, became the first golfer to exceed $3 million earnings on the US PGA Tour, without having won any of the four major championships?

9. Who, after finishing runner-up in three successive tournaments at the start of that year, had his first win on the official US PGA Tour in the 1983 Lajet Classic in Texas, and went on to help the United States win the World Cup title?

10. Who was the overseas player who won the 1948 Chicago Victory National Championship by sixteen strokes, the biggest winning margin on the US PGA Tour?

28 *The US Open Championship – Low Scoring*

1. Who was the rookie professional who, in the 1987 US Open Championship, equalled the course record at the Olympic Club, San Francisco, with a third round 64?

2. Who was the little-known golfer who finished joint second with Lanny Wadkins in the 1986 Open Championship, after closing rounds of 68 and 65?

3. Who won the 1983 US Open Championship with a tournament record total of 132 for the final thirty-six holes?

4. Who had rounds of 71, 70, 70 and 70 in the 1970 US Open Championship at Hazeltine, to be the first winner to break par and lead the tournament through every round?

5. Who led the 1981 US Open at the end of the second and third rounds with a championship record of 203 strokes for the first fifty-four holes?

6. Who had an opening round of 63 and led throughout the 1980 US Open Championship, registering a tournament record 272 strokes for seventy-two holes?

7. Who was not in the leading ten after three rounds of the 1973 US Open Championship at Oakmont, but finished with a tournament record 63 to win by one stroke?

8. Who won the 1960 US Open Championship at Cherry Hills with a then tournament record final round of 65?

9. Who led the 1985 US Open Championship for the first three rounds, equalling the tournament record of 203 strokes for the first fifty-four holes?

10. Who, in 1968, became the first golfer to score under 70 in each round of a major championship, when he won the US Open by four strokes with a total of 275 for seventy-two holes?

29 *The Australasian Tour*

1. Who was the leading American golfer who retained the New Zealand Open Championship in December 1985?

2. Who beat Greg Norman by one stroke to win the 1987 Victorian Open Championship, his only previous win having been the 1984 Western Samoan Open?

3. Who defeated Greg Norman in the quarter-final of the 1987 Australian Matchplay Championship, having previously overtaken him to win the Australian P G A Championship with a final round of 64?

4. Who won his first Australian Open Championship in November 1986?

5. Who was the last golfer to win the British Open and the Australian Open Championship in the same year, the only occasion that he was successful in either event?

6. Who, in 1984, was the last American to win the Australian Open Championship?

7. Who was the American who won the Australian Open Championship six times between 1964 and 1978?

8. Who won his only Australian Open Championship in 1960, while still an amateur?

9. Who was the British golfer who incurred a one-stroke penalty after reporting that his ball was moving as he played a stroke during the 1987 Australian Masters Championship?

10. Who was the European golfer who won a car for a hole-in-one in the 1985 Masters Tournament, on his way to a first success in Australia?

30 *The Safari Tour*

1. Who was the Englishman who won his fifth title on the Safari Tour, when he took the 1987 Zimbabwe Open after a play-off with Andrew Murray?

2. Who was the British golfer who disqualified himself from the 1987 Zambian Open by not signing his card at the end of his round, having borrowed a driver in the absence of his caddy, so breaching the maximum fourteen clubs rule for one round of golf?

3. Who was the British golfer who had his first win as a professional, at just twenty years of age, in the 1978 Nigerian Open Championship?

4. Who had his only win on the Safari Tour in the 1978 Kenyan Open, when twenty years and eleven months old?

5. Which Scottish golfer, a regular on the Safari Tour, won the Nigerian Open Championship in 1985 for the third time?

6. Who was the English golfer, in his twelfth year as a professional, who had the first win of his career with a world record low aggregate of 255 in the Nigerian Open Championship in 1981?

7. Who was the English golfer who led the 1982 Zambian Open after two rounds, but then shot an 87 and failed to qualify for the final day?

8. Who was the British Boys Champion of 1972 who won the 1985 Kenya Open, his first success as a senior?

9. Who was the Welsh golfer who won the 1985 Ivory Coast Open for his first tournament success since the 1972 Kenya Open?

10. Who was the British golfer who survived a heatwave to win both the 1986 Nigerian and Ivory Coast Open Championships in successive weeks?

31 *The British Open – Early-round Leaders*

1. Who had a first-round 64 in the 1985 Open at Royal St Georges, which contained ten birdies, seven of them in succession, four bogeys and only four holes in par?

2. Who was the young Australian who led the 1984 Open at St Andrews at the end of the second and third rounds, before falling back with a 79 in round four?

3. Who was the former US Masters Champion who led the 1983 Open at Royal Birkdale for the first thirty-six holes after rounds of 64 and 70?

4. Who was the young American who held a commanding halfway lead in the 1982 Open at Troon after rounds of 67 and 66, and remained in front in round three despite a 78, before a last day 77 relegated him to joint tenth?

5. Who was the forty-year-old former champion who led the 1980 Open at Muirfield at the halfway stage with a score of 135, before a third round 64 took Tom Watson clear of the field?

6. Who was the son of a former Wimbledon and US Men's Singles Tennis Champion who led the 1977 Open at Turnberry after a first round 66?

7. Who was the nineteen-year-old who led the field for the first sixty holes of the 1976 Open at Royal Birkdale, before finishing joint second with Jack Nicklaus?

8. Who was the South African who led the 1975 Open at Carnoustie after 54 holes, with two successive rounds of 66, before a closing 76 left him just one stroke behind Tom Watson, the championship winner?

9. In the 1969 Open Championship, who was the former champion who led Tony Jacklin by three strokes, with a halfway score of 135, before finishing runner-up, two strokes adrift?

10. Who was the American who led the 1963 Open at Lytham and St Annes, with a thirty-six hole total of 135, and ended up by losing a play-off?

32 *The European PGA Tour – Mixed Bag*

1. Who, in 1982, became the first rookie to win two events on the European Tour, with victories in the Coral Welsh Classic and the Bob Hope Classic?

2. Who is the Irish golfer who won the Spanish Open in 1983, so recording his first win on the European Tour since the 1977 Greater Manchester Open?

3. Who was the Scottish golfer who had opening rounds of 61 and 65 in the 1952 Spalding Tournament?

4. Who was the former British Ryder Cup player who had his last and most important victory on the European Tour in the 1978 Dunlop Masters?

5. Who won the 1987 Spanish Open, his first win on the European Tour since the 1984 Car Care Plan International?

6. Who started his final round in the 1987 French Open eight strokes behind the leader, but finished with five consecutive birdies for a course record equalling 63, thereby winning only his second tournament on the European Tour?

7. Which Welsh golfer completed the last thirty-six holes of the 1986 Car Care Plan International at Moortown in 129 strokes, to achieve an unexpected first win on the European Tour?

8. Who had a play-off victory over Peter Fowler in the 1986 Jersey Open for his first European success in an eighteen-year career?

9. Who, in 1986, won three European tournaments in two weeks, a sequence extended to five victories in seven weeks?

10. Who won the 1979 Cacharel World Open Under-25 Championship at Ninnes by a record margin of seventeen strokes?

33 *The WPGA Tour*

1. Who won the 1987 Eastleigh Classic with a four-round aggregate of 242, the lowest ever seventy-two hole total in a WPGA Tour event?

2. Who had her first win on the WPGA Tour in the 1987 British Open at St Mellion, having finished as runner-up on six occasions since joining the professional tour in 1984?

3. Which Briton, in 1977, was the first professional golfer to win the British Ladies Open Championship?

4. In which year did the official WPGA Tour begin?

5. Who, prior to 1987, was the last British woman to win two events in her debut season on the WPGA Tour?

6. Who won the 1985 Belgian Ladies Open for her only WPGA victory in her first season on the tour?

7. Who was the American golfer who finished joint third in the 1985 Ladies British Open and joint second in 1987?

8. Who was the French woman who won the 1987 Belgian Open in her first season as a professional?

9. Who is the famous American professional who played in the 1987 Hennessy Cognac Ladies Cup at Chantilly, but was beaten into second place by Kitrina Douglas?

10. Who was the South African golfer who won the 1979 British Ladies Open and finished as leading money winner on the circuit?

34 Men's Amateur Golf – British Performances

1. Who suffered his only first international defeat in 1981, in his twenty-sixth individual match for England?

2. Who won the President's Putter in 1985 at the age of forty-nine?

3. Who played for Scotland in the Home Internationals every year from 1961 to 1979, making five Walker Cup appearances between 1963 and 1975?

4. Who won the British Amateur Championship in 1972 and again in 1974?

5. Who finished runner-up in the British Amateur Championship for the first time in 1958 and again in 1972?

6. Who won the British Amateur Championship in 1956 at the age of eighteen years and one month, becoming the youngest-ever winner of the competition?

7. Who, in 1957, was the last Scottish-born golfer to win the British Amateur Title?

8. Who is the current leading British professional who lost the 1975 British Amateur Championship final by 8 and 7 to the American, Marvin Giles?

9. Who won the 1968 English Amateur Championship by 12 and 11 over thirty-six holes at Ganton, Scarborough, after completing the first eighteen holes in a ten under par sixty-one?

10. Who won the British Amateur Championship a record eight times between 1888 and 1912?

35 *Senior Golf*

1. Who won the inaugural Senior British Open Championship at Turnberry in 1987?

2. Who won the British PGA Seniors Championship six times between 1976 and 1983?

3. Who was the Australian who won the British PGA Seniors Championship three times between 1971 and 1975, becoming the first overseas winner of the tournament?

4. Who won the British Seniors Championship in 1967 and went on to beat Sam Snead in the World Seniors final?

5. Who was the American who at Southport and Ainsdale won the first World Seniors Championship in 1954?

6. Who was the British golfer who, in 1954, lost in the final of the first World Seniors Championship?

7. Who won the World Seniors Championship in both 1976 and 1977?

8. Who recorded a hat-trick of wins in the British PGA Seniors Championship in 1987?

9. Who was the brother of the 1939 British Open Champion who won the first British PGA Seniors Championship in 1957?

10. Who won the World Seniors Championship five times between 1964 and 1973?

36 *Mixed Bag*

1. Who is the veteran American golfer, a former winner of the US Masters, who has holed-in-one more than forty times during his long career?

2. Who, along with Jerry Heard and Bobby Nichols, went to hospital after being struck by lightning at the 1975 Western Open in Chicago?

3. Who, in January 1982, beat Severiano Ballesteros in a nine-hole play-off to win the first prize of $500,000 in the inaugural Million Dollar Sun City Challenge in Bophuthatswana?

4. Which British golfer led the 1986 Million Dollar Challenge at Sun City for three rounds but, with a closing round of 76, dropped to fifth place?

5. Which British golfer won the individual award in the 1985 Nissan Cup World Team Championship at Kapalua, Hawaii?

6. Who was the little-known golfer nominated 'Rookie of the Year' on the US PGA Tour in 1986, after finishing in seventy-fifth place on the money list?

7. Who was the World's Number One player, according to the first Sony World Rankings, issued in March 1986?

8. Which golfer, with only one prior victory on the US PGA Tour, the 1979 Quad Cities Open, finished equal third in the 1987 US PGA Championship?

9. Who was the American club golfer who won the 1985 Hong Kong Open, having failed in three attempts to win a US PGA Tour card?

10. Who was the eighteen-year-old who won the 1982 Venezuelan Open with a four-round aggregate of 272?

37 The British Open – the British Challenge

1. Who was the club professional from North Berwick who, having survived a sudden death play-off in the qualifying round, led the 1975 Open at Carnoustie with a halfway total of 136?

2. Who was the little-known English professional who tied for the lead in the 1974 Open at Lytham and St Annes with a first round 69, but fell away to finish in joint thirteenth place, and subsequently fell out of the limelight altogether until 1986, when he won his first tournament?

3. Who was the British golfer who finished joint third in the 1961 Open at Birkdale, joint second in 1973 at Troon after a last round of 66, and joint seventh in 1975 at Carnoustie, just three strokes behind the leaders?

4. Who was the British golfer who began the defence of his Open title by completing the first nine holes at St Andrews in twenty-nine strokes?

5. Who was the young Englishman, for many years the professional at Sunningdale, but more recently a television commentator, who tied for third place in the 1967 Open Championship at Hoylake?

6. Who was the American-born Welshman who finished fourth in the 1971 Open at Birkdale with a final thirty-six hole aggregate of 137?

7. On which course did Tony Jacklin win the 1969 Open Championship?

8. Who was the Briton who lost a thirty-six hole play-off with Peter Thomson for the 1958 Open at Lytham and St Annes, and finished joint second, just one stroke behind winner Jack Nicklaus, in the 1966 Open at Muirfield?

9. Who was the Scottish golfer who needed a par four at the final hole to win the 1958 Open Championship at Lytham and St Annes, but had a double-bogey six and finished joint third, one stroke behind the winner?

10. Who was the British golfer who won the Open Championship on the only occasion that it has been played on a course in Northern Ireland?

38 *The US Masters – Overseas Challengers*

1. Who were the two overseas golfers defeated in the three-man play-off for the 1987 US Masters Championship?

2. Who partnered Jack Nicklaus in his memorable final round in the 1986 US Masters Championship?

3. Who won his first and, as yet, only major title at the 1985 US Masters Championship?

4. Who celebrated his twenty-third birthday by winning the 1980 US Masters Championship, so becoming the tournament's youngest champion?

5. Who won the US Masters Championship three times in the 1960s and 1970s, a record only bettered in that period by Jack Nicklaus?

6. Who was the British golfer who led the 1973 US Masters field by three strokes after a third round of 68, before a closing 74 left him tying for third place, just two strokes behind winner Tommy Aaron?

7. Who was the British golfer who went into the final round of the 1984 US Masters Championship in third place but, after a last round of 76, slipped to joint fifteenth position?

8. Who was the young Englishman who holed in one at the sixteenth during the 1968 US Masters Championship?

9. Who was the reigning British Open Champion who missed a play-off for the 1968 US Masters Championship because he signed his card for a par four when he had, in fact, made a birdie three?

10. Who was the British golfer who completed the closing nine holes in the 1974 US Masters Championship in just thirty strokes for a record-equalling Masters round of 64, which brought him up to joint ninth place?

39 The Ryder Cup – The Captains

1. Who was playing captain of the Great Britain team in four successive Ryder Cups between 1955 and 1961?

2. Who led the American team in 1961, the last occasion on which both captains played in the competition?

3. Who was the first captain to lead Great Britain to victory in the Ryder Cup?

4. Who was Great Britain's first non-playing captain, who led his team to victory in the 1933 Ryder Cup?

5. Who were the respective captains in the 1949 Ryder Cup, the first occasion on which neither played in the competition?

6. Who was the defeated American captain in the 1957 Ryder Cup?

7. Who won both his matches in 1955, the only time that he played in the Ryder Cup, and captained the European team in both the 1979 and 1981 competitions?

8. Who was the only captain of either side never to play in the Ryder Cup?

9. Who played for Great Britain in four Ryder Cup competitions between 1953 and 1959, winning all his singles matches and losing all the foursomes, and was non-playing captain in the tied match in 1969?

10. Who was the fifty-year-old who, in 1927, captained Great Britain in the inaugural Ryder Cup competition?

40 *The European PGA Tour – Low Scoring*

1. Who won the 1987 Monte Carlo Open by just one stroke from his compatriot, Rodger Davis, with a European record-equalling aggregate of 260 for seventy-two holes?

2. Who had his first win on the European Tour with a twenty-six under par score of 262 in the 1986 Ebel European Masters in Switzerland?

3. Who, in the first round of the 1986 Jersey Open, had a ten under par score of 62, which included a European Tour record of eagle threes at all four par five holes?

4. Who recorded the lowest score of his European Tour career when opening with a score of 62 in the 1985 French Open, a round which included putts for birdies or eagles on every one of the eighteen holes?

5. Who equalled the world record of eight consecutive birdies in a round in the 1985 Benson and Hedges International at Fulford, when finishing with a 62 which leapfrogged him from twenty-second place to the runner-up position behind Sandy Lyle?

6. Who was the young Londoner who, with a first round 61, broke the course record during the 1985 Monte Carlo Open, which included a world record-equalling score of 27 for nine holes?

7. Who was the Australian who won his first event on the European Tour in the 1984 Timex Open in Biarritz, with a four-round total of 260?

8. Who won the 1983 Lawrence Batley International at Bingley, with a score of 126 for the last thirty-six holes?

9. Which continental golfer scored eleven consecutive birdies and an eagle during two rounds of the 1978 Swiss Open?

10. Who, after starting with rounds of 63 and 65, won the 1984 Glasgow Open by eleven strokes, with a seventy-two hole total of 266?

41 *The World Cup*

1. Who, representing Scotland, finished as the Individual Title runner-up in the 1984 World Cup?

2. Who was Gary Player's partner when South Africa won the World Cup in 1965 and was runner-up in 1966?

3. Who was the South African who took the Individual Title in 1974, the last occasion his country won the Team Competition in the World Cup?

4. Who is the only player to retain the Individual Title in the World Cup?

5. Who played in nineteen World Cup competitions, fifteen for Argentina and four for Mexico?

6. Who became the first golfer to play in three consecutive World Cup winning teams, when representing the United States between 1960 and 1962?

7. Which country won the inaugural World Cup in 1953, then known as the Canada Cup?

8. Who won the Individual Title in that first competition in 1953?

9. Who made six World Cup appearances for the United States between 1960 and 1967, and was in the winning team on every occasion?

10. Who was a surprise choice to partner Sandy Lyle in Scotland's team in the 1980 World Cup competition?

1. Who won the 1987 Los Angeles Open, so becoming the first golfer from Taiwan to be victorious on the US PGA Tour?

2. Who, in 1987, won the Memorial Tournament at Muirfield Village, Ohio, for only his second victory in his eleven years on the US PGA Tour?

3. Who won his first title on the US PGA Tour in the 1986 Pensacola Open, with a thirty-six-hole total of 128, the last two rounds being abandoned because of flooding?

4. Who, after entering the tournament as a qualifier, won the 1986 Southern Open in Columbus, Georgia, with an eleven under par total of 269?

5. Which famous player has never won the Canadian Open Championship, but has finished runner-up in the tournament on seven occasions?

6. Who was the fifty-five-year-old who lost the 1975 Westchester Classic in a sudden death play-off with forty-five-year-old Gene Littler?

7. Who, in 1968, became the first man to earn over $100,000 in one year on the US PGA Tour, without winning an event?

8. Who, in his first tournament for twelve months after a near fatal car crash, lost the 1950 Los Angeles Open to Sam Snead in a play-off?

9. Which early season tournament on the US PGA Tour required a play-off to find the winner every year from 1982 to 1986?

10. Who, after wins in the 1982 Quad Cities Open and the 1983 Walt Disney Classic, seemed certain to gain a third US PGA Tour success in the 1985 Byron Nelson Classic when he went into the final hole with a three-stroke lead, but a double-bogey put him into a play-off which he lost to Bob Eastwood?

43 *The US LPGA Tour*

1. Who set a record in the 1981 US Ladies Open Championship, with a four-round total of 279, completing the last thirty-six holes in 134 and making good a six-stroke deficit?

2. Who was the forty-year-old from Uruguay who, in 1955, became the first non-American and oldest winner of the US Ladies Open Championship?

3. Who won forty-four tournaments on the US LPGA Tour in four years from 1961 to 1964, heading the money list in each year?

4. Who turned professional in 1965 and took four years to win her first tournament, the 1969 US Ladies Open Championship, but was then so successful that in 1981 she became the third golfer to earn $1 million on the US LPGA Tour?

5. Who won a record five tournaments in succession in 1978, her first full season on the US LPGA Tour?

6. Who won her third US Ladies Open Championship in 1984?

7. Who won the 1985 Ladies World Championship when she beat Patty Sheehan in a play-off?

8. Who turned professional in 1979, became the first woman to win over $200,000 in a season in 1980, and exceeded $500,000 in career earnings on the US LPGA Tour before the end of 1981?

9. Who, in 1985, became the first overseas golfer to exceed earnings of $1 million on the US LPGA Tour?

10. Who is the South African golfer, a US LPGA Tour regular since 1971, who was beaten in a play-off for the 1986 US Ladies Open Championship?

44 The Open Championship – The American Challenge

1. Who was the American who won the one hundredth Open Championship at Royal Birkdale in 1971?

2. Which American golfer won five of his first nine Opens, and finished joint second in the tenth?

3. Who was the forty-year-old American who won a post-war Open at Carnoustie on his only appearance in the championship?

4. Who was the American golfer who arrived at St Andrews in 1964 for his first Open, with only enough time for one quick practice round, and went on to win the championship by five strokes?

5. Which American made just three appearances in the Open Championship between 1937 and 1962, finishing eleventh, first and sixth respectively?

6. Who followed up a surprise second place in the 1981 US Open Championship with a four-stroke victory in the British Open at Royal St George's, Sandwich?

7. Who would have won his first Open Championship in 1963 at Royal Lytham if he had played the final two holes in par fours instead of bogey fives?

8. Who was the American who finished runner-up at St Andrews in the successive Open Championships of 1939 and 1946?

9. At which Open Championship were Americans the eighth and eleventh of the first twelve?

10. Who led throughout all four rounds of the 1932 Open at Prince's, Sandwich for his only victory in the championship, in the then record low aggregate of 283?

45 *The US PGA Championship – Low Scoring*

1. Who completed all four rounds in under seventy strokes when he won the 1984 US PGA Championship?

2. Who was the forty-eight-year-old who scored a second round 63 in the 1984 US PGA Championship?

3. Who completed the first thirty-six holes of the 1983 US PGA Championship in 131 strokes, a new tournament record?

4. Who, after a record-equalling 63 in the first round, maintained his form to lead throughout the 1982 US PGA Championship?

5. Who completed the first thirty-six holes of the 1986 US PGA Championship in 133, leading the eventual winner by nine strokes?

6. Who completed all four rounds of the 1964 US PGA Championship in fewer than seventy strokes, but could only finish equal second?

7. Who won his only major title when, after a first round 64, he led throughout the 1964 US PGA Championship?

8. Who completed all four rounds of the 1979 US PGA Championship in under seventy strokes, but was beaten in a play-off?

9. Who was the Australian who, in 1975, had a record round of 63 in the US PGA Championship?

10. Who was the Australian who won the 1979 US PGA Championship after a final round of 65?

46 *The US Open Championship – Last-round Disasters*

1. Who finished the 1985 US Open Championship just one stroke behind the winner, scoring an 8 during his final round of 77, when he incurred a penalty for hitting the ball twice while fluffing a chip?

2. Who led the 1984 US Open field for the first three rounds at Winged Foot, having won the championship the last time that it was played on that course, but after a final round of 79 dropped to sixth place?

3. Who was prematurely dismissed as a 'choker' when, as a young professional, he lost a one-stroke lead in the 1974 US Open with a final round of 79, and the following year lost a halfway lead of three strokes with rounds of 78 and 77, to finish ninth?

4. Who finished just one stroke behind the winner after a last round of 78 in the 1975 US Open Championship?

5. Who led into the final round of the 1968 US Open, but finished third after shooting a 76?

6. Who was the amateur who, at the end of round three, led the 1967 US Open at Baltusrol, New Jersey, but finished equal eighteenth after a closing round of 80?

7. Who lost a seven-stroke lead, with nine holes to play, in the 1966 US Open Championship and was eventually beaten in a play-off by Billy Casper?

8. Who led the 1986 US Open field after three rounds, but dropped to twelfth position after finishing with a 75?

9. Who finished joint second in the 1981 US Open after a final round of 73, as compared with 67 for the three-stroke winner?

10. Who was the fifty-year-old who led through most of the last round of the 1920 US Open until his putting failed him during the closing holes, when he finished joint second after a final round of 78, one stroke behind compatriot Ted Ray?

47 *The European PGA Tour – British Success*

1. Who, in 1985, became the first golfer to win over £150,000 in one season on the European Tour?

2. Who played in sixty-eight tournaments on the European Tour between 1973 and 1979 without missing a thirty-six-hole cut?

3. Who won the Tunisian Open, the first event on the European Tour in 1984, and went on to become the first Scotsman to win over £100,000 in one season?

4. Which British golfer won the Portuguese and Madrid Opens in the space of three weeks in 1978, but did not win again on the European Tour until 1984?

5. Who was the twenty-year-old Scottish golfer who won his first professional tournament in 1969 and finished top of the Order of Merit?

6. Who was the forty-year-old Englishman who had seven successive birdies on his card in the second round of the 1980 Bob Hope Classic?

7. Who won the 1966 Piccadilly Strokeplay tournament at Wentworth, with a seventy-two-hole record-low aggregate for a British course of 262 strokes?

8. Who first won the News of the World Championship in 1936 and reached the final for the last time in 1969 at the age of fifty-six?

9. Who had his first professional victory on native soil in the 1986 Benson and Hedges International Open at Fulford, York, in his eleventh year on the European Tour?

10. Who, in 1986, became the first British professional to win a PGA tournament at the Belfry, when winning the Lawrence Batley event by a seven-stroke margin?

48 The Open Championship – Holes-in-one and Albatrosses

1. Who was the former English Amateur Champion who holed-in-one at Turnberry during the 1986 Open, but still failed to qualify for the final thirty-six holes?

2. Who were the three British golfers who holed-in-one during the 1981 Open at Royal St Georges?

3. Who was the British golfer who holed-in-one at Royal Birkdale in 1976, to become the first left-hander to achieve this feat in the Open?

4. Who were the two golfers, the youngest and the oldest in the field (nineteen and seventy-one years of age, respectively) who, during the 1973 Open at Royal Troon, holed-in-one at the same hole on the same day?

5. Who was the British Ryder Cup player who, in 1971 at Royal Birkdale, achieved the first televised hole-in-one at the Open championship?

6. Who was the British Ryder Cup player who holed-in-one in the 1946 Open at St Andrews, when he finished joint fourth, and performed the feat a second time in 1948 at Muirfield, where he tied for third place?

7. Who holed-in-one in the 1921 Open at St Andrews and went on to win in a play-off, the first American to win the championship?

8. Who recorded the first hole-in-one in the 1868 Open at Prestwick, in the course of winning the second of his four successive championships?

9. Who was the former champion who scored an albatross two in the first round of the 1983 Open at Royal Birkdale?

10. Who was the young American and future champion who, in 1972 at Muirfield, during a record round of 66, scored an albatross two at the 558-yard fifth hole?

49 *The US PGA Tour – Mixed Bag*

1. Who won the 1987 Hertz Bay Hill Classic to end a US Tour sequence of eight second-place finishes since 1983?

2. Who followed up his first tour win in the 1986 South West Golf Classic with third place in each of the first three tournaments in 1987, before gaining a second tour victory in the 1987 Honda Classic at Fort Lauderdale?

3. Who won the 1986 Tournament at Denver, Colorado, which used the Stableford system of scoring, with plus points for birdies and eagles and minus points for bogeys?

4. Who won the 1985 Kemper Open while wearing knee braces?

5. Who was the six foot seven inch, eighteen stones-plus Rookie of the Year who won the 1985 Greater Hartford Open?

6. What is the name of the trophy which is awarded annually to the golfer with the lowest stroke average on the US PGA Tour?

7. Who had the lowest stroke average on the US PGA Tour five times between 1960 and 1968?

8. Who, in 1974, became the first coloured golfer to win a tournament on the US PGA Tour?

9. Who reached career earnings of $1 million on the US PGA Tour in 1979, having joined the professional ranks in 1956?

10. Which tournament event on the US PGA Tour was won by Andy North in 1977?

50 *The World Matchplay Championship*

1. Who won the inaugural World Matchplay Championship in 1964?

2. Who, in 1964, became the only Briton to reach the final of the World Matchplay Championship prior to 1980?

3. Who were the two British golfers who reached the 1987 World Matchplay Final, ensuring the first-ever home victory in the event?

4. Who won a record five World Matchplay Championships between 1965 and 1973?

5. Who holed a huge putt to level with Arnold Palmer on the eighteenth green in the first round of the 1983 World Matchplay Championship, having been two down with two to play, and went on to beat the 'old maestro' at the twenty-first hole?

6. Who is the only man to play in three consecutive World Matchplay Championship finals?

7. Who reached his second World Matchplay final in three years when, in 1982, he beat Nick Faldo in the quarter-final, having been six down at halfway, and defeated Tom Kite by 8 and 7 in the semi-final?

8. Who was Nick Faldo's opponent in his first round match in the 1983 World Matchplay Championship, when a misguided 'supporter' redirected his overhit shot onto the green?

9. Who was the British golfer who holed-in-one at the par three tenth hole during the 1981 World Matchplay Championship, the first occasion this feat was performed at that green during a competition?

10. Who holed-in-one at the second hole, while playing David Graham in the 1979 World Matchplay Championship, winning himself a flat at Gleneagles?

51 *Ladies' Amateur Golf – Mixed Bag*

1. Who was the former player who captained the 1986 Great Britain and Ireland Curtis Cup Team to a first success in the competition on American soil?

2. Who, in 1964, aged seventeen, became the youngest golfer to play for the United States in the Curtis Cup?

3. Who won the 1971 American Ladies Amateur Championship at the age of sixteen years and two months?

4. Who won the British Ladies Open Amateur Championship in 1981, aged forty-five?

5. Who was the American who won the 1984 British Ladies Amateur Championship?

6. Which country won the inaugural Ladies World Amateur Team Championship in 1964?

7. Which country won the Ladies World Amateur Team Championship for the first time in 1986?

8. Which trophy is awarded to the winners of the Ladies Team Challenge involving Great Britain and Ireland against Europe, which has been held at two-yearly intervals since 1959?

9. Who won both the British Ladies Amateur Strokeplay and British Open Championships in 1978?

10. Who remains the last Briton to win the United States title, when, in 1936, she performed a double win in the British and US Ladies Amateur Championships?

52 *The Courses*

1. Which course became the most northerly championship venue in Britain when it hosted the 1985 Mens' British Amateur Championship?

2. Which championship course in the USA has a hole of only 110 yards?

3. Which course has a plaque to commemorate Arnold Palmer making the green from the middle of a bush, which was wrenched from the ground by the ferocity of his strike?

4. Which course was the venue for the first British Amateur Championship in 1885?

5. On which course is the Jersey Open played?

6. On which course is the Suez Canal hole?

7. Which course is known as the Burma Road?

8. Which British championship course has a hole called Bobby Jones?

9. Which course is known as the Ailsa?

10. Which British open championship course has a par three opening hole?

53 *The European PGA Tour – the Europeans*

1. Which tournament did nineteen-year-old Severiano Ballesteros win in 1976, so becoming the youngest winner of a European PGA Tour event?

2. Who was the Spanish player who won both the first Bob Hope English Classic in 1980 and the last in 1983?

3. Who was the teenaged Italian professional who set a European record when completing his third round in the 1971 Swiss Open in only sixty strokes?

4. Who won the Madrid and Italian Opens in consecutive weeks at the start of the 1985 European Tour?

5. Which less renowned brother had his only win on the official European Tour in the 1983 Timex Open at Biarritz?

6. Who won the 1986 Four Stars Pro-Celebrity Tournament, his first victory on the European Tour since the 1982 Tunisian Open?

7. Which 1981 tournament was made memorable by Bernhard Langer's stroke from the branches of a tree?

8. Who, in 1984, became the first non-Briton to win over £100,000 in a season on the European Tour?

9. Who, in 1986, became the first player to win over £100,000 in his rookie season on the European PGA Tour?

10. Who was the Spaniard who, after more than ten years as a professional, had his first tour win in the 1984 Lawrence Batley International, at the Belfry?

54 *Mixed Bag*

1. Who won the British Open Championship at St Andrews and described the course as 'the sort of real estate you couldn't give away'?

2. Who were the father and son who both competed in the 1982 US Open Championship, the only time that this has occurred in the tournament's history?

3. Which golfer's life was portrayed in the 1951 film, 'Follow The Sun', starring Glenn Ford?

4. Who was the amateur, later to be a narrow British Open loser, who won the 1956 Canadian Open Championship?

5. Who was the Irishman who won the inaugural Cacharel World Under 25 Championship at Evian in 1976?

6. Who, in 1951, became the first American to be elected Captain of the Royal and Ancient Golf Club?

7. Who won the 1926 News of the World P G A Matchplay title at the age of fifty-eight, and remains the oldest winner of an important tournament in Great Britain?

8. Who was the twenty-year-old who had his first professional tournament win in the 1956 Dunlop Masters at Sunningdale?

9. Who had a six-stroke lead with only three holes to play in the 1969 Alcan Golfer of the Year Championship at Portland, Oregon, but completed them in four over par and lost to Billy Casper who recorded three birdies?

10. Who scored a twenty-six under par total of 262 to win the 1981 Columbian Open by twenty-one strokes, a record margin in a national tournament?

55 *The Ryder Cup – Seasoned Competitors*

1. Who played in forty matches for Great Britain between 1961 and 1977, a record for either team in the Ryder Cup?

2. Who played in ten consecutive British Ryder Cup Teams between 1955 and 1973?

3. Who played for Great Britain in all nine Ryder Cup matches held between 1937 and 1961?

4. Who played in a record thirty-seven Ryder Cup matches for the United States between 1961 and 1975?

5. Who won a record twenty-two of his thirty-two Ryder Cup matches for the United States between 1961 and 1973?

6. Which current player has lost a record thirteen of his twenty-three Ryder Cup matches for the United States between 1969 and 1985?

7. Who played for the United States in seven Ryder Cup competitions between 1937 and 1959, and was non-playing captain in the tied match in 1969?

8. Who played in six Ryder Cup matches for Great Britain between 1963 and 1975, and was non-playing captain in 1977?

9. Who captained the United States team in all six of the Ryder Cup matches played before the outbreak of the Second World War?

10. Who played for the United States in the first six Ryder Cup matches, the only player on either side to do so?

56 *The US Masters – Low Scoring*

1. Who, after starting with a disastrous round of 79, pulled up to joint second place, just one stroke off the lead, with a record Masters round of 63 in the 1986 championship?

2. Who had a four-stroke lead halfway through the final round of the 1985 US Masters Championship, after rounds of 65 and 68 had compensated for his first round 80, before further lapses relegated him to joint second place, two strokes adrift of the winner?

3. Who won the 1976 US Masters with a record-equalling 271, completing the first two rounds in a record thirteen under par 131, and reaching the three-quarter stage in a record fifteen under par 201?

4. Who, after aggregating 146 at the halfway stage, completed the closing rounds of the 1975 US Masters in 131 strokes, to finish joint second with Tom Weiskopf, just one stroke behind the winner?

5. Who was the amateur who completed the first thirty-six holes of the 1956 US Masters in 135 to lead the field?

6. Who won his only major title at the 1959 US Masters, finishing one stroke clear after a final round of 66, which included a five under par total for the last six holes?

7. Who opened the 1940 US Masters with a round of 64, which was unequalled as the tournament record for another twenty-five years?

8. Who had successive closing rounds of 64 and 69 in the 1965 US Masters to set a championship record aggregate of 271 strokes for seventy-two holes?

9. Who set a new tournament record when aggregating 274 for seventy-two holes in the 1953 US Masters, beating the previous lowest total by a margin of five strokes?

10. Who completed the final thirty-six holes in 133 to win the 1978 US Masters by just one stroke from the trio of Rod Funseth, Hubert Green and Tom Watson?

57 *The Open Championship – Outstanding Amateur Performances*

1. Who was the teenaged Spaniard who, shortly before turning professional, finished just seven strokes behind the winner in the 1985 Open at Royal St Georges?

2. Who was the American Amateur Champion of 1980, now a leading professional, who was the only amateur to complete the seventy-two holes of the 1981 Open Championship at Sandwich?

3. Who was the British amateur who finished as the second-best home player in the 1979 Open at Royal Lytham and St Annes?

4. Who was the British amateur who held the joint lead after one round in the 1968 Open at Carnoustie, before finishing eleven strokes behind Gary Player?

5. Who was the Scottish amateur who played the first thirty-six holes of the 1966 Open at Muirfield in 141 strokes, to be just four behind the leader?

6. Who was the famous Irish amateur who looked to be a possible winner of the 1960 Open at St Andrews after 54 holes, but finished eighth, seven strokes behind the winner, after a final round of 73?

7. Who was the Scottish amateur who led the eventual winner at the start of the final round in the 1959 Open at Muirfield, before finishing joint fifth, four strokes behind the winner?

8. Who was the English golfer who had a closing round of 68 to finish sixth in the 1960 Open at St Andrews, with a record low championship total for an amateur of 283?

9. Who was the almost unknown Scottish amateur who finished fifth in the 1957 Open at St Andrews, equalling or beating par in every round?

10. Who was the popular American amateur who finished second in the Opens of 1947 and 1953 at Hoylake and Carnoustie?

58 *The European WPGA Tour*

1. Who made a winning debut as a professional at the 1984 Ford Ladies Classic at Woburn?

2. Who was the Japanese golfer who won the 1984 British Ladies Open Championship by eleven strokes?

3. Who was the forty-five-year-old American, with eighty-six wins on the United States Tour, who had her first success in Europe in the 1984 Ladies Irish Open Championship?

4. Who was the Scottish professional who won over £28,000 on the 1984 WPGA Tour, at that time a record in European Ladies golf?

5. Who won the WPGA Order of Merit in both 1985 and 1986, her first two years on the European Tour?

6. Who began her professional career with a play-off victory in the 1985 Ford Ladies Classic at Woburn, having a repeat success in 1987?

7. Who, in 1976, won the inaugural British Ladies Open Golf Championship while still an amateur?

8. Who was the British professional who won £10,000 for a hole-in-one in the 1983 United Friendly Championship at Worthing?

9. Who collected the winner's cheque when she finished third behind two amateurs in the 1984 European Ladies Championship at the Belfry?

10. Who was the nineteen-year-old Swedish girl who, in 1985, became the youngest-ever winner on the WPGA Circuit when she won the Hoganas Open in Sweden, followed by the European Open at Kingswood Country Club in Surrey?

59 Men's Amateur Golf – Britain in the Walker Cup

1. Who was the only Briton to win both his singles matches in the 1987 Walker Cup?

2. In the 1983 Walker Cup, who became the first Briton, and only the second player in the history of the event, to win all four of his matches?

3. Who played for Great Britain and Ireland in the 1981 Walker Cup match aged seventeen years and seven months, the youngest-ever competitor?

4. Who was seventeen years and ten months when he played for Great Britain and Ireland in the 1985 Walker Cup?

5. Who captained the victorious Great Britain and Ireland team in the 1971 Walker Cup match?

6. Which member of the Great Britain and Ireland team in 1987 first played in the Walker Cup in 1971, when he won both his matches?

7. Which famous course has hosted the Walker Cup on both the occasions when Great Britain and Ireland have won the competition?

8. Who played in ten Walker Cup matches for Great Britain and Ireland between 1947 and 1967?

9. Who captained the winning Great Britain and Ireland Walker Cup team in 1938?

10. Who were the two brothers who played together for Great Britain and Ireland in the 1932 Walker Cup Team?

60 *The European PGA Tour – British Success*

1. Who was the Englishman who, in 1979, became the first golfer to reach £200,000 career winnings in Europe?

2. Who was the Englishman who, in 1983, became the first golfer to win more than £100,000 in one season on the European Tour?

3. Who won the 1974 Scandinavian Open by a record eleven strokes?

4. Who was the nineteen-year-old who, in his first full season as a professional, won the 1982 Dutch Open Championship?

5. Who, in 1986, won the Madrid Open for the third time in his career?

6. Who was the English golfer who won the Portuguese Open in 1985, his first victory in his fourteenth year as a professional?

7. Who was the twenty-one year-old who, with a 65 in his final round, won the 1979 European Open by a clear seven strokes?

8. Who was the young Englishman who, in 1985, had his first tournament victory, winning the Cannes Open after a play-off with David Llewellyn?

9. Who, in winning the 1985 Monte Carlo Open, equalled the European Tour record for thirty-six holes with an aggregate score of 125 for the second and third rounds?

10. Which Ryder Cup golfer climaxed twenty-four consecutive rounds of par or better by winning the 1968 French Open Championship?

61 *The US Open Championship – Mixed Bag*

1. Who was the rookie who won the 1976 US Open Championship at the Atlanta Athletic Club?

2. Who won the US Open in 1974, and again in 1979, though on both occasions he was over par for his final round?

3. Who has won the US Open Championship by the post-war record margin of seven strokes?

4. Who was the future dual winner of the US Open who finished fifty-fourth in 1966, his first appearance in the championship as an unknown twenty-six-year-old?

5. Who, after winning his last major title in 1964, finished third, fourth and fifth in consecutive US Open Championships between 1972 and 1974?

6. Who was the forty-seven-year-old who finished with a six and a seven at the 1960 US Open, when two fours would have given him the championship for a record fifth time?

7. Who was the forty-three-year-old who won his second US Open in 1963, eleven years after his first success in the championship?

8. Who, in 1956, was the reigning British Open Champion who, on a then rare visit to America, finished fourth in the US Open Championship?

9. Who was the pre-tournament qualifier who won the 1969 US Open Championship for his only victory on the US PGA Tour?

10. Who was the coloured American who, after qualifying for the tournament for the first time, proceeded to lead the 1981 US Open Championship with a round of 66?

62 *The US LPGA Tour*

1. Who was the great all-round sportswoman who won the 1954 US Ladies Open Championship by twelve strokes on her last appearance in the event?

2. Who won the US Ladies Open Championship on four occasions between 1958 and 1964?

3. Who won the 1949 US Ladies Open Championship by a record fourteen strokes, her only victory in the event, though she was runner-up four times between 1955 and 1963?

4. Who won seventeen of her first fifty tournaments after turning professional?

5. Who was the Japanese golfer who became the first overseas winner of the US LPGA Championship in 1977?

6. Who won four US Ladies Open Championships between 1951 and 1960?

7. Who was the forty-three year-old who, in 1982, became the first golfer to win over $300,000 in a season in the US LPGA Tour?

8. Who was the leading money-winner on the US LPGA Tour in eight years out of nine between 1965 and 1973?

9. What does the golfer with the lowest stroke average on the US LPGA Tour receive each year?

10. Who won the first US Ladies Open Championship in 1946, the only occasion on which matchplay was adopted, and in a successful career, became the first player to win $100,000 on the US LPGA Tour?

63 *The US PGA Tour – Mixed Bag*

1. Who, in 1976, the year before winning the US Open, became the tenth golfer to win three tournaments in succession on the US PGA Tour?

2. Who won at least one tournament on the US PGA Tour every year from 1937 to 1961?

3. Who was the tournament qualifier who won the 1980 Phoenix Open, the last to do so before 1986?

4. Which tournament on the US PGA Tour coincides with the British Open Championship?

5. Who had his first win in ten years on the US PGA Tour in the 1985 San Diego Open?

6. Who followed a creditable performance in the 1987 US PGA Championship with a three-round victory in the rain-affected Western Open, his second win in ten years as a tour professional?

7. Who won the 1987 US PGA Order of Merit, earning a record $925,941 on the year's tour?

8. Who achieved the thirty-second tournament victory of his career, but his first since 1984, when winning the 1987 Nabisco Championship at San Antonio?

9. Who won the 1987 Tucson Open, so ending eleven years of frustration during which he became the first golfer on the US PGA Tour to exceed $1 million in career earnings without winning an event?

10. Who, in 1980, became the first golfer to win more than $500,000 in one season on the US PGA Tour?

64 *The Open Championship – the First, the Last, the Only*

1. Who is the only left-handed player to win the Open Championship?

2. Who was the last player to win the Open Championship in three different decades?

3. Who, in 1946 at St Andrews, won the first post-war Open Championship?

4. Who was the last player to win the Open in an eighteen-hole play-off?

5. Who, when winning the 1939 Open, remains the last Briton to win the championship at St Andrews?

6. Who was the last player to win the Open with a seventy-two-hole total in excess of par?

7. Who, in 1907 at Hoylake, was the first overseas player to win the Open Championship?

8. Who, in 1922 at Sandwich, was the first American-born player to win the Open Championship?

9. Who, in 1927 at St Andrews, became the first overseas player to successfully defend the Open Championship?

10. Who was the last player to win the Open Championship three times in succession?

65 *The US PGA Championship – Mixed Bag*

1. Who won his only major title when he took the 1967 US PGA Championship, beating Don Massengale in a play-off, having previously been beaten himself in a play-off in 1961 at the hands of Jerry Barber?

2. Who was the Australian runner-up in both the 1973 and 1975 US PGA Championships?

3. Who was the Australian who won the 1947 US PGA Championship, beating Chick Harbert 2 and 1 and, thirteen years later, was runner-up, one stroke behind the winner?

4. Who was the forty-seven-year-old who had a five-stroke advantage halfway through the final round of the 1977 US PGA Championship, but took forty-one strokes for the inward nine holes, and was subsequently beaten in a sudden death play-off?

5. Who was the forty-eight-year-old who won the 1968 US PGA Championship, becoming the oldest player to win the title?

6. Who was the sixty-two-year-old who finished joint third in the 1974 US PGA Championship at Tanglewood, three strokes behind the winner?

7. Who won the US PGA Championship in 1953, the year in which Ben Hogan won the other three major titles?

8. In which year did the US PGA Championship switch from a matchplay to strokeplay competition?

9. Who won the last US PGA Championship which was contested under matchplay conditions?

10. Who was beaten in the final of the last matchplay US PGA Championship and, the following year, won the first stroke-play title?

66 *The Major Championships*

1. Which current golfer has won the British Open, the US Open and the US Masters at least once, and has also contested a play-off for the US PGA Championship?

2. Which previous US Masters Champion is the youngest winner of the British Open Championship this century?

3. Who was the Cornish-born, naturalized American, who won the US PGA, the US Open and the British Open Championships on at least one occasion each between 1916 and 1925?

4. Who, in 1983, was the first in a sequence of eighteen consecutive major championships which were won by eighteen different golfers, a sequence he himself ended in 1987?

5. Who won all three major US championships at least once between 1937 and 1945, but only competed twice in the British Open, finishing fifth in 1937, and well down in 1955, fifteen strokes behind the winner?

6. Who was the last golfer to win the US Open and the British Open Championship in the same year?

7. Who has created an all-time record by playing in over one hundred consecutive major championships?

8. Which player created a record by winning the British Open, the British Amateur Championship, the US Open and the US Amateur Championship all in the same year?

9. Who was the last non-American to hold the British and US Open Championships at the same time?

10. Who is the only golfer to win two different major championships before his twenty-first birthday?

67 *The Australasian Tour*

1. Who won the New Zealand Open in 1954 as an eighteen-year-old amateur?

2. Who was the American Ryder Cup player who had his first win in Australia in the 1986 Masters Tournament?

3. Which Australian golfer won his first New Zealand Open Championship in 1963 and his second in 1984?

4. Which Australian golfer won himself a town house for holing-in-one at the 1981 Tooth Classic Tournament in Queensland?

5. Who was the young Australian who won his first professional tournament in the Victorian PGA Championship in November 1986 and, a month later at La Manga in Spain, led the qualifiers for the 1987 European Tour?

6. Who has won the Australian Open Championship on a record seven occasions?

7. Who had his first win as a professional in the 1976 Australian West Lakes Classic?

8. Who won the Australian PGA Championship four times between 1946 and 1951, and the Australian Open Championship three times between 1950 and 1953?

9. Who was the British golfer who won the 1980 Australian PGA Championship?

10. Which European golfer had his only win in Australia in the 1981 PGA Championship?

68 Men's Amateur Golf – the Americans

1. Who successfully defended the United States Amateur Championship in 1983?

2. Who was the son of a famous father who surprisingly won the 1981 United States Amateur Championship?

3. Who is the current leading professional who, in 1980, won the United States Amateur Championship by 9 and 8 over thirty-six holes, in addition to taking the Individual Title in the World Amateur Team Championship by nine strokes?

4. Who won the United States Amateur Title in 1959 aged nineteen, and was successful again in 1961 before turning professional?

5. Who was the 1953 United States Amateur Champion who turned professional in 1954 and, in the same year, finished second in the US Open Championship at Baltusrol?

6. Who was the American who lost three British Amateur Championship finals between 1959 and 1970, the last two in successive years to Michael Bonallack?

7. Who was the American who, in 1967, won the British and United States Amateur Championships in the same year, the last time that this has been achieved?

8. Who was the American who won the British Amateur Championship at Prestwick in 1934 by a record 14 and 13, and the United States Championship by 8 and 7?

9. Who was the American who won the British Amateur Championship for the second time in 1950, but was beaten in the United States Championship at the thirty-ninth hole?

10. Who beat Bobby Jones by 8 and 7 in the semi-final of the 1922 United States Amateur Championship, his worst defeat in either the American or British events, and became the first American-born winner of the British Championship in 1926?

69 *The European PGA Tour – Mixed Bag*

1. Who was the South African who won the Order of Merit and the Vardon Trophy on the European PGA Tour in 1975?

2. Who, in 1969, was the last American to be the leading money winner on the European PGA Tour?

3. Which famous golfer had his last tournament win in the 1982 PGA Championship?

4. Who was the young Canadian who had his first win on the European PGA Tour in the 1984 Swiss Open, with a tournament record 261 for the seventy-two holes?

5. Who finished second in the 1984 British Open and won the Dutch and Irish Open Championships, all in a period of fourteen days?

6. Which British golfer made his professional debut in the 1984 British Open Championship and completed the seventy-two holes in level par to tie with Jack Nicklaus in thirty-first place?

7. Who was the famous American golfer who had his only European tournament win at the 1955 French Open Championship?

8. Who was the Welsh golfer who had his last PGA Tour win in the 1978 Jersey Open?

9. Who was the thirty-one-year-old who had his first win on the European Tour in the 1985 Car Care Plan International Tournament at Moortown, Leeds?

10. Who was the last Irishman to win the Irish Open Championship in 1982?

70 *The Open Championship – Mixed Bag*

1. Who won his first open championship by two strokes in 1959 at Muirfield, despite a double bogey at the last hole, after having started his final round in joint tenth position?

2. Who finished third in the 1977 Open at Turnberry, ten strokes behind runner-up Jack Nicklaus?

3. Who was the British golfer who finished joint third in the 1962 Open at Royal Troon, despite being thirteen strokes behind the winner?

4. Who was the reigning US Open Champion who led the 1979 Open at Royal Lytham and St Annes after the second and third rounds, but finished sixth after a final round of 78?

5. Who was the Scottish golfer who played the first nine holes of the 1979 Open at Royal Lytham in twenty-nine strokes, completing his first round in 65 for a three-stroke lead, but eventually finished well down the field, his final round being an 82?

6. What is the name of the trophy which is awarded each year to the British player with the lowest round in the Open Championship?

7. Who was the only player to win the Open Championship both before and after the Second World War?

8. Who was the British professional who finished fourth in the Opens of 1928 and 1929 and third in 1931, while based at the Wansee Golf Club in Berlin?

9. Who was the four-time Open Champion who died at the age of twenty-four?

10. Who was the four-time post-war Open winner who finished his first championship in 1936 at Hoylake in eighth place as the leading amateur?

71 The US Masters – Last-round Disasters

1. Who, seeking his first major title in his thirteenth year on the US PGA Tour, went into the final round of the 1984 US Masters with a one-stroke lead, but scored a 75 and finished equal sixth?

2. Who started the last round of the 1979 US Masters with a five-stroke lead, but bogeyed the last three holes and lost the championship in a three-way sudden death play-off?

3. Who led the 1969 US Masters by one stroke until he bogeyed the last three holes and finished fifth, but later went on to win the title in 1971?

4. Who had a final round of 80 in the 1956 US Masters, losing the championship by one stroke?

5. Who was the Australian who led the 1950 US Masters by five strokes with just six holes to play, but lost by two after a disastrous sequence of dropped shots?

6. Who was the defending champion who went into the final round of the 1959 US Masters six strokes ahead of the eventual winner, but finished third after a round of 74?

7. Who was the reigning US Open Champion who started the final round of the 1978 US Masters with a three-stroke lead over the whole field and a seven-stroke margin over the eventual winner, but who missed a short putt for a play-off on the last green and was forced to settle for a three-way tie for second place?

8. Who had a final round of 75 in the 1954 US Masters and lost a play-off to Sam Snead who had finished with a 72?

9. Who led Byron Nelson by four strokes after fifty-four holes of the 1937 US Masters, but finished two strokes behind him after a final round of 76?

10. Who bogeyed the last hole in the 1986 US Masters to finish equal second, one stroke behind the winner, after having led at the start of the final round?

72 Ryder Cup – Mixed Bag

1. Which of the 1987 Ryder Cup captains had a direct role in the competition for the tenth time in the last eleven matches?

2. Who won all nine of his Ryder Cup matches in 1979 and 1981?

3. Who made his debut for the United States in the 1985 Ryder Cup, and lost all three of his matches?

4. Which current player had his first Ryder Cup victory in his eleventh match, ending a sequence of eight defeats and two halves?

5. Which is the only Scottish course to have played host to the Ryder Cup?

6. On which course did Great Britain win the 1957 Ryder Cup?

7. Who was the last playing captain of either team in the Ryder Cup?

8. Who were the brothers who played for Great Britain in the 1963 Ryder Cup?

9. Who are the only father and son to have played in the Ryder Cup?

10. Who were the brothers who played in separate Ryder Cup matches for the United States between 1957 and 1961?

73 Mixed Bag

1. Who had his best year on the US PGA Tour in 1985 when he won both the Westchester Classic and the World Series of Golf, his first victories since the 1976 Dublin Memorial Tournament?

2. Who, prior to 1987, had his only win on the US PGA Tour in the 1983 Memphis Classic?

3. Which major 1987 winner had his first win on the US PGA Tour in the 1980 Western Open?

4. Who is the only golfer to win the US Open, the Canadian Open and the British Open Championships in the same year?

5. Who is the only Australian to win more than one of America's three major professional tournaments?

6. Which tournament opened the European PGA Tour from 1982 to 1985?

7. Which Briton won the 1987 Swedish Open by two strokes, with a nine under par sixty-three, after starting the final round five behind?

8. Who were the brothers who both finished in the first eight in the 1987 US PGA Championship?

9. Who was the amateur who won the 1945 Memphis Open and also became the first American to play in both the Walker and Ryder Cups?

10. Who, in 1928, lost a seventy-two-hole challenge match by 18 and 17 to Britain's Archie Compston, and in his next tournament won the British Open Championship?

74 *The US PGA Tour – Winning Sequences*

1. Who won four tournaments in 1986, his first victories in three years on the US PGA Tour?

2. Who won the first three tournaments on the 1974 US PGA Tour and completed the season with eight victories?

3. Who had eleven consecutive wins on the US Tour in 1945?

4. Who heads the list of winners on the US Tour, with eighty-four victories in nearly thirty years?

5. Who became the eleventh player to win three tournaments in succession on the US PGA Tour in 1978, aged forty-two?

6. Who had fifty-one career wins on the US PGA Tour, including three tournament victories in a row in 1960?

7. Who won at least one tournament on the US PGA Tour every year from 1955 to 1973?

8. Who won seven events on the US PGA Tour in both 1972 and 1973?

9. Who won thirteen events on the US Tour in 1946 and a further eleven in 1948?

10. Who won four consecutive US Tour events in three weeks during February and March 1952?

75 *The US Open Championship – Mixed Bag*

1. Who lost a play-off for the 1975 US Open Championship and held a substantial lead in the final round the following year, before finishing joint fourth?

2. Who won his only US Open Championship to date at Pebble Beach in 1982?

3. Who was the little known golfer who came second in the 1974 US Open Championship and, later in the year, won the Southern Open for his only US PGA Tour success?

4. Who was the controversial American golfer who finished second to Tony Jacklin in the 1970 US Open Championship?

5. Who was the unknown club golfer who had a last round of 67 in the 1955 US Open Championship to tie with Ben Hogan, and then won the play-off for his first win in sixteen years as a professional?

6. Who was the last man to successfully defend the US Open Championship?

7. Which US Open course, last used in 1981, is the shortest in the championship, with a yardage of 6544 and a par of seventy?

8. Who played in fifteen US Open Championships between 1940 and 1960, during which his lowest position was tenth, his worst round was 77 and his highest aggregate was 294?

9. Who twice won the US Open Championship, relegating Jack Nicklaus to second place on both occasions?

10. Who finished second in the 1980 US Open Championship at Baltusrol, New Jersey, with a seventy-two hole total of 274 strokes, the lowest score to date by a runner-up in the tournament?

76 The Open Championship – Mixed Bag

1. Who won the Centenary Open Championship in 1960?

2. Who was the Irishman who tied with Bobby Locke after seventy-two holes in the 1949 Open at Sandwich, despite having to play from beside a broken bottle on one occasion?

3. Who was forced to play left-handed from beside the Club House wall after overshooting the final green at Royal Lytham in 1974, but still had no problem in securing a four-stroke victory?

4. Who won his only Open Championship by six strokes in 1976, after starting his final round in second place?

5. Who has held the record lowest score of 132 for the first thirty-six holes of the Open Championship for more than fifty years?

6. Who won an Open Championship at Hoylake with the highest winning post-war total of 293, which included a single round score of 78?

7. Who was the unheralded British club professional who led the 1959 Open for three rounds before finishing equal second?

8. Who was the Taiwanese who finished a close second in the 1971 Open at Royal Birkdale?

9. Who 'killed off' his playing partner and main challenger, Tony Jacklin, by chipping directly into the hole on the seventy-first green in the 1972 Open at Muirfield?

10. Who, in 1982 at Royal Troon, achieved the highest-ever position by a Japanese golfer in the Open Championship, when finishing joint fourth, just two strokes behind Tom Watson?

77 The European PGA Tour – the Commonwealth and South African Invasion

1. Who had his first two wins in Europe in the Martini International Tournaments of 1977 and 1979?

2. Who had his first European victory since 1981 when he won the 1986 Whyte and Mackay PGA Championship at Wentworth, in spite of a bogey six at the third extra hole of a play-off with Des Smyth?

3. Who had his first success on the European PGA Tour in the 1985 Scandinavian Open?

4. Who was the South African who won the 1986 Portuguese Open, his first European Tour success, with an eighteen under par total of 270?

5. Who, in 1985, won both the Lawrence Batley Tournament and the Dutch Open immediately before and after the Open Championship at Sandwich, in which he finished joint twentieth, six shots behind the winner?

6. Who was the Australian who won the 1984 German Open for his first tournament win since 1978, a period in which he was runner-up on seventeen occasions?

7. Who won the 1981 English Classic at the Belfry, having finished as runner-up in fourteen tournaments since his previous win in the 1979 Victorian Open?

8. Who was the South African who won the 1986 Cannes Open, the first event of that season's European Tour?

9. Who was the young New Zealander (whose two brothers are also international sportsmen) who had his first European success in the 1986 Scandinavian Open?

10. Who was the young South African who beat Severiano Ballesteros in the semi-final of the 1987 Epson Grand Prix Matchplay Tournament at St Pierre, Chepstow?

78 Ladies' Amateur Golf – Mixed Bag

1. Who was the French winner of the 1969 British Ladies Open Amateur Championship?

2. Who was the sixteen-year-old who reached the final of the 1986 English Ladies Closed Championship?

3. Who was the seventeen-year-old who, in 1986, became the youngest winner this century of the British Ladies Amateur Championship?

4. Who remains the youngest British Ladies Amateur Champion, having won the event in 1899 at the age of seventeen years and one week?

5. Who won the American Ladies Amateur Championship three times in successive years between 1980 and 1982?

6. Who, between 1922 and 1935, won the United States Ladies Amateur Championship on a record six occasions?

7. Who won the 1986 United States Ladies Amateur Championship by 9 and 7, the most one-sided victory in a final for twenty-four years?

8. Who are the only mother and daughter to win the British Ladies Open Amateur Championship?

9. Who, in 1946, won her only American Ladies Amateur Championship by 11 and 9, before embarking on a successful, but tragically brief, professional career?

10. Who is the American professional who won the United States Ladies Amateur Championship five times between 1957 and 1968?

79 *The World Matchplay Championship*

1. Who lost to Gary Player in the semi-final of the 1965 World Matchplay Championship, after being seven strokes ahead with seventeen holes to play?

2. Who is the only man to have beaten Gary Player in a World Matchplay final?

3. Who won the 1970 World Matchplay Championship, his only success in three final appearances?

4. Who was the American golfer who won the 1979 World Matchplay Championship, beating Isao Aoki in the final?

5. Who became the first Australian to win the World Matchplay Championship in 1976?

6. Who was the Australian who took Gary Player to the fortieth hole in the 1973 World Matchplay final?

7. Who was the New Zealander who reached the 1978 World Matchplay final?

8. Who was the 1969 World Matchplay Champion who lost to Nick Faldo in the semi-final of the competition fourteen years later?

9. Who were the British and American players who shared eighteen birdies and four eagles in their 1973 World Match-play encounter?

10. Who, in 1986, made his first appearance in the World Matchplay Championship for fifteen years, and was eight under par when winning his opening match against Jose-Maria Olazabal at the thirty-second hole?

80 *The Open Championship – Consistent Performers*

1. Who finished third, third and second between 1948 and 1950, but had to wait until 1967 for his only Open Championship win?

2. Who has finished runner-up in the Open Championship a record seven times in sixteen years?

3. Who was the British golfer who finished second in the Open Championship in 1953, 1954 and 1961?

4. Who finished in the first two in seven consecutive Open Championships between 1952 and 1958?

5. Who finished second, first and first again in his first three Open Championships, but has never subsequently finished higher than seventh?

6. Who was the British golfer who finished first, second and twice third in the Open Championship in the years between 1947 and 1952?

7. Who was the Belgian who finished runner-up twice and was in the first ten in eight Open Championships between 1950 and 1959 ?

8. Who was the British Ryder Cup golfer who finished joint third in the 1939 Open, joint fourth in 1949, and joint fifth in 1959?

9. Who was the British golfer who finished third in the 1934 Open Championship, second in 1935 and first in 1936?

10. Who was the Australian golfer who finished in the first five in the Open Championship six times between 1960 and 1966?

81 *The US PGA Tour – Young and First-time Winners*

1. Who was the twenty-one-year-old US Amateur Champion who won the 1985 Western Open after a play-off with Jim Thorpe?

2. Who was the twenty-nine-year-old qualifier who won the 1986 Honda Classic at Fort Lauderdale, Florida?

3. Who won the 1982 Walt Disney Classic for his first win on the US Tour just months after becoming a professional?

4. Who made a successful professional debut in 1973 by winning the Texas Open?

5. Who is the current tour player who won the 1963 St Petersburg Open aged twenty years and five months?

6. Who won the 1955 Canadian Open, his first professional tournament?

7. Which future US Open Champion won the 1954 San Diego Open while still an amateur?

8. Who, in his fourth year on the US PGA Tour, had his first victory in 1979 when, just short of his thirty-sixth birthday, he won the Greater Milwaukee Open?

9. Who won the 1985 Greater Greensboro Open, his first tournament victory, in his second year on the US PGA Tour?

10. Who had his first US tour win in the 1986 Memphis Classic at the Colonial Country Club in Tennessee, when he beat former school-friend Joey Sindelar by one stroke?

82 *The European PGA Tour – Mixed Bag*

1. Who was the British golfer who was disqualified after completing his second round in the 1984 European Open at Sunningdale, when a film recording showed that he had unintentionally dropped his ball in the wrong place at a water hazard?

2. Who won the 1982 European Open at Sunningdale with a last round of 63, which included just thirty strokes for the inward nine holes?

3. Who won the now discontinued PGA Matchplay Tournament in 1964, 1965 and 1973?

4. Who won a British Ryder Cup place in 1979, having won his only European Tour victory in that year's Tournament Players Championship?

5. Who won a £55,000 car for a first-round hole-in-one at the 1985 Monte Carlo Open?

6. Who was the Australian who, in 1947, set a record which has still not been surpassed, when he won three of the first four, and four of the first six tournaments on that year's European Tour?

7. Who was the Spanish golfer, uncle of Severiano Ballesteros, who, in 1971, became the first player to be fined by the PGA for slow play on a British course?

8. Who, after winning the 1981 Sun Alliance PGA Championship at Ganton, Scarborough, was fined for slow play, along with his playing partners, Ken Brown and Greg Norman?

9. Who had his first win on the European Tour in the 1980 Dunlop Masters at St Pierre, Chepstow?

10. Who had his only win to date on the European Tour, in the inaugural 1984 Monte Carlo Open, with a thirty-six hole total of 131, after the tournament had been reduced because of bad weather?

83 Men's Amateur Golf – Mixed Bag

1. Who was the Frenchman who, in 1981, became the first golfer from the Continent to win the British Amateur Championship?

2. Who, between 1983 and 1985, achieved a unique treble by winning the British Boys, the British Amateur and the British Youth Championships in successive years?

3. Who was the South African who became the first overseas golfer to win the English Open Amateur Strokeplay Championship in 1974?

4. Who was the twenty-four-year-old South African who led throughout the 1986 Brabazon Trophy at Sunningdale, to win by four strokes?

5. Who, in 1949, was the last Ulsterman to win the British Amateur Title prior to 1985?

6. Who were the two young golfers who shared the 1985 English Amateur Strokeplay Championship?

7. Who played for the United States in the 1985 Walker Cup, ten years after his brother, who is now a successful professional on the US PGA Tour?

8. Who are the only father and son to play for Great Britain and Ireland in the Walker Cup?

9. Who represented England at Boy, Youth and Full International level in 1976, prior to winning the 1978 English Amateur Championship?

10. Who played for the United States in the 1987 Walker Cup at the age of eighteen and won both his matches?

84 *The Dunhill Nations Cup*

1. When was the Dunhill Nations Cup first played?

2. Which course is used for the Dunhill Nations Cup Competition?

3. Who beat Spain, the pre-tournament favourites, in the second round of the 1985 Dunhill Nations Cup?

4. Which country surprisingly beat England in the first round of the 1986 Dunhill Nations Cup?

5. Which country scored a surprise victory over the United States to reach the 1986 Dunhill Nations Cup Final?

6. Which country won the Dunhill Nations Cup in both 1985 and 1986?

7. Who won all his matches in the Dunhill Nations Cup in both 1985 and 1986?

8. Which country won the 1987 Dunhill Nations Cup, having previously never progressed beyond the second round of the competition?

9. Who shot a round of 64 in the 1987 Dunhill Nations Cup final?

10. The course record was broken twice during the 1987 Dunhill Nations Cup, once when Rodger Davis scored a 63 for Australia against Canada in a quarter-final match, and subsequently when which player achieved a round of 62 against Australia in the third-place play-off?

85 *The US Senior Tour*

1. Who was the fifty-year-old Australian who won seven tournaments on the US Senior Tour in 1986, to be the leading money winner?

2. Who was the fifty-six-year-old Australian who won nine tournaments on the US Senior Tour in 1985, to be the leading money winner?

3. Who, during March 1986, his first month as a senior, won two tournaments on the US Tour, and lost another in a play-off?

4. Who had his first win on the US Senior Tour in the PGA Championship at Palm Beach in February 1986, just three months after his fiftieth birthday?

5. Who is the popular Puerto Rican golfer who has recently enjoyed great success on the US Senior Tour?

6. Which golfer, the leading money winner on the US Senior Tour in both 1982 and 1983, has won at least two tournaments each year on the tour since 1981?

7. Who was the former English Walker Cup player who won more than $90,000 on the US Senior Tour in 1983?

8. Who was the overseas golfer who won nearly $60,000 on the US Senior Tour in 1986, at the age of sixty-three?

9. Who won only three tournaments in a twenty-two-year career on the US PGA Tour, but, in 1983, won two events in his first year on the US Senior Tour?

10. Who was the Commonwealth golfer who reached his fiftieth birthday in March 1986 and won over $260,000 in the next nine months on the US Senior Tour?

86 *The World Cup*

1. Who was the European golfer who won the Individual Title in the 1960 World Cup, aged forty-eight, and continued to play in the competition until 1979, when he was sixty-seven?

2. Who were the brothers who represented Spain in the 1958 World Cup and finished runners-up in the team event, one winning the individual competition?

3. Which pair won the 1958 World Cup team competition for Ireland?

4. Who was the fifty-one-year-old who partnered Sam Snead for a United States victory in the 1961 World Cup?

5. Which course hosted the event in 1956, the only occasion that it has been played in England?

6. Who were the English players who were runners-up in the team competition in the 1960 World Cup?

7. Which country was the surprise winner of the 1972 World Cup competition in Melbourne?

8. Who was Peter Thomson's partner when Australia won two World Cup competitions, as well as finishing runners-up twice, between 1954 and 1961?

9. Who were the Australians who won the 1970 World Cup competition?

10. Who partnered Bob Shearer in Australia's team in the 1976 World Cup, although he had only played in six tournaments since turning professional earlier in the year?

87 The Open Championship – the First, the Last, the Only

1. Who, in 1978, became the first player since James Braid in 1910 to win a second Open Championship at St Andrews?

2. Who was the first player to win an Open Championship in under 270 strokes?

3. Who, in 1931 at Carnoustie, was the last Scottish-born player to win the Open Championship?

4. Who is the only American to win an Open Championship at Royal Lytham?

5. Who was the last Briton to win the Open Championship on more than one occasion?

6. Who won the first Open Championship at Prestwick in 1860?

7. Who won the last Open Championship to be held at Prestwick in 1925?

8. Who, in 1977 at Turnberry, became the first player to complete a round in 63 strokes at an Open Championship?

9. Who is the only player to score a record-equalling round of 63 on the way to winning an Open Championship?

10. Who won the first Open to be held at St Andrews in 1873?

88 *The European PGA Tour – the Americans*

1. Who had his first victory in Europe in the 1985 Swiss Open, beating David Feherty and Ove Sellberg by two strokes?

2. Who was the forty-five-year-old who won the 1985 Dunhill Masters at Woburn, beating Rodger Davis by three strokes?

3. Who won the 1980 European Open at Walton Heath for his first overseas win?

4. Which holder of the US Masters won the Alcan Golfer of the Year Championship at St Andrews in 1967, retaining the title at Royal Birkdale the following year?

5. Who, in September 1973, won the WD & HO Wills Tournament in Birmingham and the John Player Classic at Turnberry, his only two victories in Europe?

6. Who won both the Spanish Open and the PGA Championship in 1975, when he was nearly forty-six years old?

7. Which less famous brother won the inaugural Panasonic European Open at Walton Heath in 1978?

8. Which European Tournament, played annually on the outskirts of Paris, was won on seven occasions by American golfers between 1971 and 1980?

9. Who was the young American who won the 1976 Irish Open at Portmarnock?

10. Who was the young American who finished fourth on the 1977 European Order of Merit, after winning the Dutch and Scandinavian Open Championships?

89 *The Major Championships*

1. Who, in 1986, was the leader or joint leader at the end of the third round in all of the four major championships?

2. Which current golfer has twice won the British Open, the US Open, and the US PGA Championships, but has never finished higher than tenth in the US Masters?

3. Which current American golfer had finished second or third at least once in all four major championships before winning any of them?

4. Who is the only non-American to win all four major championships?

5. Who, in 1900, became the first golfer to win both the British and US Open Championships?

6. Who was the first golfer to win both the British and US Open Championships in the same year?

7. Who lost an eye in the First World War, but overcame his handicap to win the US Open, the US PGA and the British Open Championships between 1927 and 1931?

8. Who, in 1922, became the first golfer to win the British Open, the US Open and the US PGA Championships?

9. Who won the British Open, the US Masters and the US PGA Championships at least once and was four times runner-up in the US Open?

10. Who had his only major victory in the British Open, finished runner-up in the US Masters four times was second and twice third in the US Open and came third in the 1975 US PGA Championship?

90 *The South African Tour*

1. Who won the South African Open Championship thirteen times between 1956 and 1981?

2. Who won the 1986 South African Open Championship after finishing as runner-up in his five previous tournaments?

3. Who won the South African PGA Championship in 1986 with a record fifteen under par total of 265 for his first success on the circuit since the 1980 South African Open?

4. Who was the South African who, having established himself on the US PGA Tour, returned home for only his second win on the South African circuit with a one-stroke margin in the 1986 Goodyear Classic in Port Elizabeth?

5. Who won seven of the eleven tournaments on the 1987 South African Tour?

6. Who was the forty-five-year-old golfer from Soweto who led the field with a first round 65 in the 1987 Wild Coast Sun Classic, the first event on the South African Tour, but had really achieved his best performance when winning the 1976 French Open Championship?

7. Who was the English-born golfer who won the South African Open Championship eight times between 1925 and 1952?

8. Who had his first win in South Africa in the 1981 Sun City Classic at the Gary Player Country Club in Johannesburg?

9. Who was the leading American golfer who won the 1973 South African P G A Championship?

10. Who was the South African who won the P G A Championship three years in succession between 1965 and 1967?

91 *The US PGA Tour – Overseas Winners*

1. Which non-American was the leading money winner on the 1986 US PGA Tour?

2. Who, in 1961, became the first overseas golfer to be the season's leading money winner on the US PGA Tour?

3. Who was the overseas player who won seven tournaments in the USA in 1947, and finished second in that season's money list?

4. Who, in 1977, was the first overseas player to win the US Rookie of the Year award, aged thirty-three?

5. Who, in 1983, became the second overseas golfer to win the Rookie of the Year award on the US PGA Tour?

6. Who had his first successes on the US PGA Tour in 1984 when, in six weeks, he won the Buick Open, the World Series and the Las Vegas Invitational?

7. Who, in 1972, became the first overseas player to win $1 million on the US PGA Tour?

8. Who won the 1985 Sea Pines Heritage Classic for his second victory in the United States within seven days?

9. Who won the 1978 Greater Greensboro Open for his first success on the US PGA Tour?

10. Who won the 1963 Houston Open, so becoming the first left-handed golfer to win an event on the US PGA Tour?

92 *Men's Amateur Golf – Expert Mixed Bag*

1. Who was the famous amateur golfer who, in 1911, became the only Briton to win the British and American Amateur Championships in the same year?

2. Who is the only man to have won the British and United States Amateur Championships in successive years?

3. Which country won the first World Amateur Team Championship in 1958?

4. Who completed his four rounds in the 1960 World Amateur Team Championship in a record low aggregate of 269?

5. Which country, in 1984, won its first World Amateur Team Championship in Hong Kong?

6. Which Australian became the first overseas winner of the British Amateur Championship in 1904 at Sandwich?

7. Which two members of the United States winning four in the 1980 World Amateur Team Championship have subsequently won the US PGA Championship on the professional circuit?

8. Which country won the first two biennial competitions for the European Team Championships?

9. How many players from each country comprise a team in the Home International Championship?

10. Which amateur competition is scored by discarding each day's poorest individual round of the team members?

93 *The Open Championship – Expert Mixed Bag*

1. Who was the English amateur who, in 1897, won his second Open Championship when it was held for the first time on his home course at Hoylake?

2. Who was the young English amateur who tied for first place in the 1921 Open at St Andrews after seventy-two holes?

3. Who was the twenty-one-year-old, already the winner of US Open and PGA Championships, who entered his first Open Championship in 1923 at Troon, but was eliminated at the qualifying stage?

4. Who was the Argentinian who started the final round of the 1931 Open at Carnoustie, three strokes ahead of the field and five ahead of Tommy Armour, who was to win with a round of 71?

5. Who won the 1923 Open at Troon to record the last English success before Henry Cotton's first victory in 1934?

6. Who won the 1904 Open at Sandwich to become the first champion to complete the championship in under 300 strokes?

7. Who was the former crane driver who took 121 strokes to complete eighteen holes of a qualifying round for the 1976 Open Championship?

8. Who was the golfer who lost an all-American play-off for the 1933 Open at St Andrews?

9. Which Scottish course was used as an open venue for the sixth and last time in 1889?

10. Who was the only golfer to win two British Open Championships in play-offs?

94 *The US Open Championship – Expert Mixed Bag*

1. Who won the 1964 US Open Championship after qualifying for the tournament for the first time in four years?

2. Who never won the US Open Championship, but finished second in 1937, lost a play-off by one stroke in 1947, was second again in 1949 and 1953, and tied for third place in 1955?

3. Who, in 1933, was the last amateur to win the US Open Championship, finishing one stroke ahead of Ralph Guldahl at the North Shore Golf Club?

4. Who finished first or second eight times in nine consecutive US Open Championships?

5. Who won the 1931 US Open Championship by one stroke from the former amateur George von Elm, after a play-off over seventy-two holes, the match being extended beyond the then normal thirty-six extra holes because the scores were still level?

6. Which American, renowned for his quick temper and club throwing, won the 1988 US Open at Southern Hills Country Club in Oklahoma, his only success in a major championship?

7. Who was the Cornish-born naturalised American who won the 1921 US Open Championship by a twentieth century record margin of nine strokes?

8. Who, in 1911, not only became the first native-born American to win the US Open Championship, but, aged nineteen years and ten months, remains the youngest title holder?

9. Who won the US Open Championship four times between 1948 and 1953?

10. Who, in 1937 and 1938, won consecutive US Open Championships, a feat that has since been repeated on just one occasion?

95 *The US Masters – Expert Mixed Bag*

1. Who never won the US Masters Championship, but finished joint second in 1969, 1972, 1974 and 1975?

2. Who was the defending champion who had a hole-in-one and a triple bogey at successive holes in the first round of the 1972 US Masters?

3. Who was the defending champion who double bogeyed the seventy-second hole at the 1961 US Masters, when a par would have earned him a place in a play-off?

4. Who made up an eight-stroke deficit on the third round leader to win the 1956 US Masters Championship?

5. Who never won any of the other major titles, but became the first three-time winner of the US Masters with victories in 1940, 1947 and 1950?

6. Who finished second, second and first in successive US Masters Championships between 1937 and 1939?

7. Who was the fifty-four-year-old, twice a champion, who equalled his best-ever round in the US Masters with a third-round 66 in 1967, his twenty-fifth and final appearance in the championship?

8. Who finished equal second in the 1969 US Masters, having led the tournament, but won the following year by beating Gene Littler in a play-off?

9. Who, in 1975, became the first competitor in the US Masters to complete the opening nine holes in only thirty strokes?

10. Who was the forty-nine-year-old who equalled the existing record with a round of 64 in the 1979 US Masters Championship?

96 *The US PGA Championship – Expert Mixed Bag*

1. Who won the US PGA Championship four years in succession from 1924 to 1927, beating, in turn, Jim Barnes, Bill Mehlhorn, Leo Diegel and Joe Turnesa?

2. Who was the thirty-four-year-old who won his first major title in the 1946 US PGA Championship, beating Porky Oliver 6 and 4?

3. Who are the only brothers to win the US PGA Championship?

4. Who was the former US and Wimbledon Men's Singles Champion who reached the semi-final of the 1951 US PGA Championship?

5. Who, in 1916 and 1919, won both the first and second US PGA Championships?

6. Who beat Sam Snead by a record 8 and 7 in the 1938 US PGA matchplay final?

7. Which twenty-one-year-old retained his US PGA title in 1923?

8. Who played in five of the six US PGA Championship finals held between 1939 and 1945, winning two and losing three?

9. Who won the 1965 US PGA championship, his only major title, and in the same year made his debut in the Ryder Cup?

10. Which golfer, with a penchant for nearly winning major championships, finished second and twice third in consecutive US PGA Championships between 1959 and 1961?

97 The US Open Championship – Expert Low Scoring

1. Who shared a record-equalling opening round of 63 in the 1980 US Open at Baltusrol, but finished the championship in thirty-sixth position?

2. Who equalled the course record with a third round 64 in the 1981 US Open at Merion, but could only finish the championship in joint eleventh position?

3. Which unknown golfer had a final round of 67 in the 1936 US Open, overcoming a four-stroke deficit and winning the championship with a then record low aggregate of 282?

4. Who began the 1968 US Open with rounds of 67 and 68 for a then championship record total of 135 for thirty-six holes, eventually finishing third, due to a final round of 76?

5. Who was the little-known club professional who had a second-round 65 in the 1973 US Open after entering the championship as a last-minute replacement for the indisposed Dave Hill?

6. Who was the virtual unknown who returned a then US Open record 64 in the second round of the 1966 Open Championship at the Olympic Country Club, San Francisco?

7. Who won the 1932 US Open with a final round of 66, which was to remain the lowest closing round to win the championship for twenty-eight years?

8. Who had a second round of 64 in the 1964 US Open, leading the championship field until the final round when a 76 launched him into second place?

9. Who was the amateur who finished second in the 1960 US Open Championship with a four-round total of 282 strokes?

10. Who became the first golfer to break 70 in the final round of the US Open when, in 1922, he finished with a 68 to win the championship by one stroke?

98 *The US Masters – Expert Mixed Bag*

1. Who was the amateur who finished equal second in the 1947 US Masters Championship, tying with 1942 champion Byron Nelson?

2. Who was the amateur who finished third in the 1954 US Masters, just one stroke behind Sam Snead and Ben Hogan?

3. Who was the amateur who finished joint second in the 1961 US Masters, just one stroke behind Gary Player?

4. Who was the Spanish golfer who finished sixth in the 1965 US Masters, at that time the highest placing by a European?

5. Who, recording his only win in the championship in 1941, became the first golfer to lead the US Masters in all four rounds?

6. Who, in 1967, became the first defending champion to fail to make the cut for the last thirty-six holes of the US Masters?

7. Who won the inaugural US Masters Championship in 1934?

8. Who won the 1935 US Masters on his first appearance in the championship, so becoming the first winner of all four major professional championships?

9. Who, in a three-way play-off, won the 1979 US Masters, the first time that he had qualified to play in the championship?

10. Who finished runner-up in both the first two US Masters Championships?

99 *The Open Championship – Expert Mixed Bag*

1. What was donated by Prestwick Golf Club for the early winners of the Open Championship, until it became the property of Tom Morris Jnr in 1870 after his third win in succession?

2. Who had his first and last Open victories at Royal Birkdale, being the only champion to win more than one of the six championships staged at this venue?

3. Who was the legendary golfer who finished in the first two in the Open Championship eleven times between 1894 and 1914, with five wins and six seconds?

4. Who was the Scottish-born golfer who won the 1920 Open Championship, despite being thirteen strokes behind at halfway, after successive rounds of 80, thus becoming the last man to win a major with a round of 80 on his card?

5. Who was the Scottish-born golfer who had his only open win in 1902, was runner-up for the first time in 1892 and for the last time in 1920, and continued to play in the championship until 1939?

6. Who was the Scottish-born golfer who won five Open Championships between 1901 and 1910?

7. Which was the first English course to stage the Open Championship?

8. What was the surname of the three English brothers who all finished in the first three in an Open Championship during the inter-war years?

9. Who, in 1890, was the first amateur to win the Open Championship?

10. Who was the English-born South African who finished runner-up to Henry Cotton in the 1934 Open Championship?

100 *The US Open Championship – Expert Mixed Bag*

1. Who were the two famous British golfers who lost in a three-man play-off for the 1913 US Open Championship by five and six strokes respectively?

2. Who was the unknown twenty-year-old amateur who won this play-off for the 1913 US Open Championship, entering the tournament only because it was near his home?

3. Who was the amateur who won the 1915 US Open Championship and never played in the tournament again?

4. Who was the Scottish-born golfer who won the 1906 US Open Championship, beating his younger brother Willie by seven strokes, and who won again in 1910 by beating his youngest brother Macdonald in a three-man play-off, also involving John McDermott?

5. Who was the local professional, born in England, who won the first-ever US Open Championship at Newport, Rhode Island in 1895?

6. Who won the 1899 US Open Championship at Baltimore by the tournament record margin of eleven strokes?

7. Who finished fourth in his first US Open in 1913, just one stroke off a play-off, but led throughout the following year to win the championship, aged twenty-two?

8. Which golfer, in a period of seven years, both won and lost twice when involved in four play-offs for the US Open Championship?

9. Who won the US Open Championship four times in five years between 1901 and 1905, and in the process, became the only man to win the tournament in three consecutive years?

10. Who, in 1916, won the US Open Championship and the US Amateur Title, the first man to win both in the same year?

101 *1988 Open Championship*

1. Who began the 1988 Open Championship at Royal Lytham and St Annes with birdies at each of the first three holes, finishing with a 67 to hold the lead after the first round?

2. Who was the only player to break par in all four rounds of the Open Championship?

3. Who, with a third round of 67, won the Tooting Bec Cup for the lowest round by a home player in the 1988 Open Championship?

4. Who was the twenty-two-year-old holder of the Lytham Trophy who had a four round total of 296 in the Open Championship, the only Amateur player to survive the half-way cut?

5. Who started his third round with a hole-in-one, the only such instance at the 1988 Open Championship?

6. Which British qualifier, playing with Jack Nicklaus, missed a hole-in-one at the start of his third round by inches, but birdied six of the first nine holes to reach the turn in 29, the lowest outward nine in the Championship?

7. Which 52-year-old, a past winner and runner-up in Open Championships at Royal Lytham, displayed a continuing affection for the course with a final score just three strokes over par?

8. Who ended the second round of the Open Championship sharing third place with Nick Faldo, but slipped towards the rear of the field after a disastrous third round of 81, ten over par?

9. Which two players shared fourth place, the leading Americans in the 1988 Open Championship?

10. Which member of the 1983 American Walker Cup team shot a first round 69 in the 1988 British Open to share second place with Australia's Wayne Grady, eventually finishing eleventh, equal with a level par aggregate?

102 *1988 US Masters and US Open Champion-ships*

1. Who birdied the final hole, in spite of driving into a bunker, so winning the 1988 US Masters Championship by one stroke?

2. Who, having already completed his round, was probably anticipating victory, or at least a play-off, when the above birdie relegated him to second place in the tournament?

3. Who barely survived the half-way cut in the 1988 US Masters, his total of 150 being twelve strokes off the lead, but finished the Championship in equal fifth place, just four strokes adrift, after shooting a last round 64?

4. Which British golfer, in his first US Masters, made an early exit from the Championship after disappointing rounds of 81 and 74?

5. Which leading American golfer had a hole-in-one at the US Masters, the first since 1972, but was never in serious contention and finished the Championship eleven strokes behind the winner?

6. Who missed the half-way cut in the 1988 US Open, as he had done in 1963, the previous time that the Championship had been held at the Country Club, Brookline?

7. Who was the leading Amateur in the 1988 US Open Championship, just nine strokes behind the winner, with a three over par aggregate of 287?

8. Who was the defending champion who equalled the US Open record with an outward nine of 30 in his second round 66, thereby taking the half-way lead in the Championship?

9. Which American golfer, whose only Ryder Cup appearance was at the Belfrey in 1985, had a final round of 64 at the US Open, just one stroke over the championship record?

10. Who, with approximately $3½ million earnings on the US Tour in a twelve-year professional career, finally won a major championship with a four-stroke margin over Britain's Nick Faldo in an eighteen hole play-off for the 1988 US Open?

103 *1988 European Tour*

1. Who was the twenty-six-year-old from County Durham who, just three months after finally gaining his tour card, won the Barcelona Open after a four man play-off with fellow Britons, Nick Faldo, Barry Lane and Mark Mouland?

2. Who, the month after winning the Zambia Open, won the Biarritz Open by a seven-stroke margin with a European record total of 258 which included a record-matching 60 in the third round?

3. Who, with rounds of 76 and 78 at the Cannes Open, missed his first 36 hole cut in a European tournament since the Sanyo Open in 1982?

4. Which 32-year-old Warrington club professional won the Madrid Open, his first tournament victory in a professional career beginning in 1979?

5. Who won the £50,000 first prize in the Epson Grand Prix Match Play at St Pierre, scoring a comfortable 4 and 3 victory over Mark McNulty?

6. Which young British player, seeking his first victory on the European tour, had opening rounds of 63 and 64 in the Spanish Open at Pedrena, his 127 total being just one stroke outside the European record, but unfortunately failed to maintain this momentum in the closing rounds and finished third, four strokes behind winner Mark James?

7. Who, when winning the Dunhill British Masters at Woburn, became only the second player to exceed £1 million in prize money on the European tour?

8. Which surprise absentee from the US Open won the concurrent European event, the Belgian Open, his first tournament victory since 1986?

9. Which former Club Professional Champion led the French Open with a first round 65, retaining his position until Nick Faldo eagled the seventy-second and last hole to pip him for the championship by two strokes?

10. Which British golfer had his first win on the European tour with a thirteen-under-par total of 271 in the Bell's Scottish Open at Gleneagles, beating a field considerably strengthened by overseas players acclimatising for the following week's Open Championship?

1. Who became the first American to win the President's Putter when registering a 4 and 3 victory over 52-year-old Ted Dexter in the latter's sixth defeat in seven final appearances?

2. Who pipped fellow Irishman Eamonn Darcy in the Lexington PGA Tournament, Johannesburg, the first overseas winner on the Sunshine Circuit since 1985?

3. Who achieved his second and third successes on the US PGA tour, in the same city, in a period of five weeks, accomplishing a three round win in the storm-affected Tournament of Champions and a one-stroke victory in the San Diego Open?

4. Who became the first Swedish golfer to win the British Amateur Championship, his one-hole victory over South African Ben Fouchee climaxing the first final between overseas players since 1981?

5. Which 24-year-old son of a former Ryder Cup player had his first significant success as a professional when winning the 1988 Kenya Open?

6. Whom did Sandy Lyle defeat in a 'sudden death' play-off for the 1988 Phoenix Open, his bogey five being good enough to earn him his third victory on the US PGA tour?

7. Who overcame the disappointment of having only a non-playing role in Great Britain's victorious 1988 Curtis Cup team, by reaching the semi-final of the British Amateur Matchplay Championship?

8. Who ended ten years on the US Tour without a victory, in spite of seven second place finishes, with a four-stroke win in the 1988 Los Angeles Open and, getting a taste for victory, proceeded to win the New Orleans Open by seven strokes, his 26 under par total of 262 being just one off the tour record of 27, shared by Ben Hogan and Mike Souchale?

9. Who was the Fijian golfer whose victory in the Nigerian Open and second and third place finishes in the Zimbabwe and Kenyan Opens made him the leading money winner on the 1988 Safari tour?

10. Whom did Sandy Lyle defeat in a play-off when winning the 1988 Greater Greensborough Open, so becoming the first Briton to win two US tour events in one season?

Answers

1 The 1987 Ryder Cup
1. Jose-Maria Olazabal   2. Nick Faldo and Ian Woosnam
3. Severiano Ballesteros   4. Dan Pohl   5. Eamonn
Darcy   6. Larry Nelson   7. The Fourballs   8. Ben
Crenshaw   9. Severiano Ballesteros   10. Europe 15,
United States 13

2 The 1987 British Open Championship
1. Nick Faldo   2. Paul Azinger   3. Rodger Davis
4. Gerard Taylor   5. Craig Stadler   6. Arnold Palmer
7. Paul Mayo   8. Ian Woosnam   9. Billy Andrade
10. Tom Watson

3 The World Matchplay Championship
1. Wentworth   2. Bernhard Langer   3. Greg Norman
4. Rodger Davis   5. Sandy Lyle and Tommy Nakajima
6. Isao Aoki, 1978   7. Twelve (eight non-seeds play in the
first round and four seeds enter in round two)   8. Peter
Thomson   9. Ben Crenshaw   10. Hale Irwin and Al
Geiberger

4 The European PGA Tour – Mixed Bag
1. Howard Clark   2. Anders Forsbrand   3. Sam
Torrance   4. Mark O'Meara   5. Paul Way   6. Nick
Faldo   7. Severiano Ballesteros (Cannes, Madrid and Italian
Opens)   8. The Lancôme Trophy   9. Isao Aoki
10. Mark McNulty

5 Men's Amateur Golf – British Performances in Major Championships
1. David Curry   2. Garth McGimpsey   3. Philip Parkin
4. Michael Bonallack   5. Ian Hutcheon   6. Peter
McEvoy   7. Guy Wolstenholme   8. Joe Carr   9. Clive
Clark   10. Michael Bonallack, Rodney Foster, Michael
Lunt and Ronnie Shade

6 The US PGA Tour – British Performances
1. Sandy Lyle   2. Ken Brown   3. Nick Faldo   4. Sam
Torrance   5. Nick Faldo   6. Peter Oosterhuis   7. Tony
Jacklin   8. Henry Cotton   9. Dai Rees   10. Peter
Oosterhuis

7 The US Open Championship: Overseas Challengers
1. Sandy Lyle   2. Tony Jacklin   3. Peter Oosterhuis
4. Greg Norman   5. David Graham   6. Gary Player
7. Bruce Crampton   8. Kel Nagle   9. Severiano
Ballesteros   10. Tze-Chung Chen

8 Mixed Bag
1. The US Masters   2. The British Open Championship
trophy   3. The winners of the Women's World Amateur
Team Championship   4. The Royal and Ancient Golf Club
of St Andrews   5. Michael Bonallack   6. Deane Beman
7. Ken Schofield   8. Colin Snape   9. Frank Hannigan
10. Bobby Jones

9 The British Open – the British Challenge
1. Gordon J. Brand   2. Ian Woosnam   3. Royal St
Georges, Sandwich   4. Denis Durnian   5. Peter
Oosterhuis   6. Sandy Lyle   7. Mark James   8. Gordon J.
Brand   9. Carl Mason   10. Peter Oosterhuis

10 The US Masters – Mixed Bag
1. Larry Mize   2. Jack Nicklaus   3. Ben Crenshaw
4. David and Danny Edwards   5. Greg Norman   6. Gary
Player   7. Jack Newton   8. Bobby Cole (South Africa)
9. Bruce Crampton   10. Jack Nicklaus, 1966

11 The Ryder Cup – British and European Successes
1. Manuel Pinero   2. Peter Oosterhuis   3. Brian Barnes
4. Bernard Gallacher   5. Dai Rees   6. Bernhard Langer
and Paul Way   7. Harry Weetman   8. Sid Easterbrook
9. George Duncan   10. Sam King

12 The European WPGA Tour
1. Cathy Panton   2. Dale Reid   3. Patricia Johnson
4. Penny Grice-Whittaker   5. Laura Davies   6. Dale
Reid   7. Corinne Dibnah   8. Laura Davies   9. Peggy
Conley   10. Debbie Massey

13 The US PGA Championship – Mixed Bag
1. Bob Tway   2. Jack Nicklaus   3. Raymond Floyd,
champion in 1969 and 1982   4. Arnold Palmer
5. Billy Casper   6. Lee Trevino, 1984   7. Lanny
Wadkins   8. Dave Stockton   9. John Mahaffey
10. Tom Watson

14 *The Open Championship – Last-round Spectaculars*
1. Severiano Ballesteros   2. Graham Marsh   3. Tom
Watson   4. Johnny Miller   5. Gary Player   6. Jack
Nicklaus   7. Peter Allis   8. Bernard Hunt   9. Ben
Hogan   10. Bobby Locke

15 *The European PGA Tour – Mixed Bag*
1. Ian Woosnam   2. Gordon Brand Jnr   3. Bernhard
Langer   4. Severiano Ballesteros, who reached this target
in 1986   5. Mark McNulty   6. Nick Faldo   7. Ian
Woosnam   8. Mark James   9. Jose-Maria Canizares
10. Antonio Garrido

16 *The US PGA Tour – Mixed Bag*
1. Dewey Arnette   2. Robert Wrenn   3. Curtis Strange
4. Severiano Ballesteros   5. Craig Stadler   6. Corey
Pavin   7. Jesse Snead   8. Tom Watson   9. Tucson Open
Championship   10. Greg Norman

17 *The US LPGA Tour*
1. Patricia Bradley   2. Jane Geddes   3. Patricia Bradley
4. Nancy Lopez   5. Kathy Whitworth   6. Judy Rankin
7. Kathy Baker   8. Jan Stephenson (Australia)   9. Joanne
Carner   10. Catherine Lacoste

18 *The World Cup*
1. Howard Clark   2. Ian Woosnam   3. Tom Kite and
Lanny Wadkins   4. Sandy Lyle   5. Severiano Ballesteros
6. David Llewellyn (Wales)   7. Spain   8. Gary Player
9. Philippines   10. Scotland

19 *The US Open Championship – Mixed Bag*
1. Scott Simpson   2. Tom Watson   3. Raymond Floyd
4. Denis Watson (South Africa)   5. Fuzzy Zoeller
6. Andy North   7. Lou Graham   8. Arnold Palmer
9. Jack Nicklaus   10. Cary Middlecoff

20 *Ladies' Amateur Golf – British Performances*
1. Patricia Johnson   2. Belle Robertson   3. Mary
McKenna   4. Penny Grice   5. Brigitte Varangot
6. Gillian Stewart   7. Jill Thornhill   8. Patricia Johnson
9. Fiona MacDonald   10. Joyce Wethered

21 *The Courses*
1. The Belfry   2. Royal Troon, sixth hole   3. St Andrews,

first and eighteenth holes   4. Royal Blackheath; The
Society of Blackheath Golfers was formed in 1608
5. Carnoustie   6. Gleneagles   7. Muirfield   8. The 126-
yard eighth hole at Royal Troon ('The Postage Stamp')
9. Hoylake   10. Royal Birkdale

22 The Open Championship – the American Challenge
1. Tom Watson at Royal Birkdale   2. Ben Crenshaw
3. Jack Nicklaus   4. Billy Casper   5. Doug Sanders
6. Arnold Palmer, 1962   7. Hale Irwin   8. Tom
Weiskopf   9. Phil Rodgers   10. Densmore Shute

23 The South African Tour
1. Mark McNulty   2. Chris Williams   3. Gavin
Levenson   4. Paul Way   5. Corey Pavin   6. Tommy
Horton   7. Tony Johnstone   8. Charlie Bolling   9. Bobby
Locke   10. Mark McNulty

24 The Ryder Cup – Youngest and Oldest Competitors and Firsts
1. Paul Way   2. Hal Sutton   3. Antonio Garrido
4. 1979   5. Jose Rivero   6. Brian Waites   7. Nick Faldo
8. Don January   9. Peter Butler   10. Royal Birkdale

25 Mixed Bag
1. Ian Woosnam   2. Lanny Wadkins   3. Severiano
Ballesteros   4. Graham Marsh   5. Greg Norman
6. Arnold Palmer   7. Jack Nicklaus   8. The Penina
Course on the Algarve, Portugal   9. South Herts   10. Bill
Shankland

26 The European PGA Tour – British Success
1. Ian Woosnam   2. Nick Faldo   3. Brian Waites
4. Peter Alliss   5. Bernard Gallacher   6. Steve Bennett
7. Sandy Lyle   8. Tony Jacklin   9. Peter Oosterhuis
10. Ken Brown

27 The US PGA Tour – Mixed Bag
1. Paul Azinger   2. Keith Clearwater   3. Don Pooley
4. Isao Aoki   5. Al Geiberger   6. Johnny Miller   7. Sam
Snead   8. Tom Kite (equalled later in the year by Curtis
Strange)   9. Rex Caldwell   10. Bobby Locke

28 The US Open Championship – Low Scoring
1. Keith Clearwater   2. Chip Beck   3. Larry Nelson
4. Tony Jacklin   5. George Burns   6. Jack Nicklaus

7. Johnny Miller 8. Arnold Palmer 9. Tze-Chung Chen 10. Lee Trevino

29 The Australasian Tour
1. Corey Pavin 2. Roger Mackay 3. Mike Harwood
4. Rodger Davis 5. Bill Rogers, 1981 6. Tom Watson
7. Jack Nicklaus 8. Bruce Devlin 9. Sam Torrance
10. Bernhard Langer

30 The Safari Tour
1. Gordon J. Brand Snr 2. Brian Barnes 3. Sandy Lyle
4. Severiano Ballesteros 5. Bill Longmuir 6. Peter
Tupling 7. David J. Russell 8. Garry Harvey 9. David
Llewellyn 10. Gordon J. Brand

31 The British Open – Early-round Leaders
1. Christy O'Connor Jnr 2. Ian Baker-Finch 3. Craig
Stadler (USA) 4. Bobby Clampett 5. Lee Trevino
6. John Schroeder (USA) 7. Severiano Ballesteros
8. Bobby Cole 9. Bob Charles (New Zealand)
10. Phil Rodgers

32 The European PGA Tour – Mixed Bag
1. Gordon Brand Jnr 2. Eamonn Darcy 3. Tom
Haliburton 4. Tommy Horton 5. Nick Faldo 6. Jose
Rivero 7. Mark Mouland 8. John Morgan
9. Severiano Ballesteros 10. Bernhard Langer

33 The WPGA Tour
1. Patricia Johnson 2. Alison Nicholas 3. Vivien
Saunders 4. 1979 5. Kitrina Douglas, 1984 6. Laura
Davies 7. Muffin Spencer-Devlin 8. Marie-Laure
Taya 9. Nancy Lopez 10. Alison Sheard

34 Men's Amateur Golf – British Performances
1. Peter McEvoy 2. Ted Dexter 3. Charlie Green
4. Trevor Homer 5. Alan Thirlwell 6. John Beharrell
7. Reid Jack 8. Mark James 9. Michael Bonallack
10. John Ball

35 Senior Golf
1. Neil Coles 2. Christy O'Connor Snr 3. Kel Nagle
4. John Panton 5. Gene Sarazen 6. Percy Alliss
7. Christy O'Connor Snr 8. Neil Coles 9. John Burton
10. Sam Snead

36 *Mixed Bag*
1. Art Wall   2. Lee Trevino   3. Johnny Miller
4. Howard Clark   5. Sandy Lyle   6. Brian Claar
7. Bernhard Langer   8. D. A. Weibring   9. Mike Aebli
10. Ronan Rafferty

37 *The British Open – the British Challenge*
1. David Huish   2. John Morgan   3. Neil Coles   4. Tony
Jacklin, 1970   5. Clive Clark   6. Craig Defoy   7. Lytham
and St Annes   8. Dave Thomas   9. Eric Brown   10. Max
Faulkner, 1951

38 *The US Masters – Overseas Challengers*
1. Greg Norman and Severiano Ballesteros   2. Sandy
Lyle   3. Bernhard Langer   4. Severiano Ballesteros
5. Gary Player   6. Peter Oosterhuis   7. Nick Faldo
8. Clive Clark   9. Roberto de Vicenzo   10. Maurice
Bembridge

39 *The Ryder Cup – the Captains*
1. Dai Rees   2. Jerry Barber   3. George Duncan, 1929
4. John Henry Taylor   5. Charles Whitcombe and Ben
Hogan   6. Jack Burke Jnr   7. John Jacobs   8. John
Henry Taylor   9. Eric Brown   10. Ted Ray

40 *The European PGA Tour – Low Scoring*
1. Peter Senior (Australia)   2. Jose-Maria Olazabal
3. Gordon J. Brand   4. Severiano Ballesteros   5. Ian
Woosnam   6. Robert Lee   7. Mike Clayton   8. Nick
Faldo   9. Jose-Maria Canizares   10. Ken Brown

41 *The World Cup*
1. Gordon Brand Jnr   2. Harold Henning   3. Bobby
Cole   4. Jack Nicklaus, 1964   5. Roberto de Vicenzo
6. Sam Snead   7. Argentina   8. Tony Cerda
(Argentina)   9. Arnold Palmer   10. Steve Martin

42 *The US PGA Tour – Mixed Bag*
1. Tze-Chung Chen   2. Don Pooley   3. Ernie Gonzalez
4. Fred Wadsworth   5. Jack Nicklaus   6. Julius Boros
7. Frank Beard   8. Ben Hogan   9. The Bob Hope Classic
10. Payne Stewart

43 *The US LPGA Tour*
1. Patricia Bradley   2. Fay Crocker   3. Mickey Wright

4. Donna (Caponi) Young   **5.** Nancy Lopez   **6.** Hollis
Stacy   **7.** Amy Alcott   **8.** Beth Daniel   **9.** Jan
Stephenson   **10.** Sally Little

44 *The Open Championship – the American Challenge*
1. Lee Trevino   **2.** Tom Watson   **3.** Ben Hogan   **4.** Tony
Lema   **5.** Sam Snead   **6.** Bill Rogers   **7.** Jack Nicklaus
8. Johnny Bulla   **9.** Turnberry, 1977   **10.** Gene Sarazen

45 *The US PGA Championship – Low Scoring*
1. Lee Trevino   **2.** Gary Player   **3.** Hal Sutton
4. Raymond Floyd   **5.** Greg Norman   **6.** Arnold Palmer
7. Bobby Nichols   **8.** Ben Crenshaw   **9.** Bruce
Crampton   **10.** David Graham

46 *The US Open Championship – Last-round Disasters*
1. Tze-Chung Chen   **2.** Hale Irwin   **3.** Tom Watson
4. Frank Beard   **5.** Bert Yancey   **6.** Marty Fleckman
7. Arnold Palmer   **8.** Greg Norman   **9.** George Burns
10. Harry Vardon

47 *The European PGA Tour – British Success*
1. Sandy Lyle   **2.** Neil Coles   **3.** Sam Torrance
4. Howard Clark   **5.** Bernard Gallagher   **6.** Brian
Waites   **7.** Bernard Hunt   **8.** Dai Rees   **9.** Mark James
10. Ian Woosnam

48 *The Open Championship – Holes-in-one and Albatrosses*
1. Andrew Oldcorn   **2.** Gordon J. Brand, Roger Chapman
and Sam Torrance   **3.** Peter Dawson   **4.** David J. Russell
and Gene Sarazen   **5.** Lionel Platts   **6.** Charlie Ward
7. Jock Hutchinson   **8.** Tom Morris Jnr   **9.** Bill Rogers
10. Johnny Miller

49 *The US PGA Tour – Mixed Bag*
1. Payne Stewart   **2.** Mark Calcavecchia   **3.** Ken Green
4. Bill Glasson   **5.** Phil Blackmar   **6.** The Vardon
Trophy   **7.** Billy Casper   **8.** Lee Elder   **9.** Don January
10. The Westchester Classic

50 *The World Matchplay Championship*
1. Arnold Palmer   **2.** Neil Coles   **3.** Ian Woosnam and
Sandy Lyle   **4.** Gary Player   **5.** Severiano Ballesteros
6. Hale Irwin, 1974–1976   **7.** Sandy Lyle   **8.** Graham
Marsh   **9.** Brian Barnes   **10.** Isao Aoki

51 Ladies' Amateur Golf – Mixed Bag
1. Diane Bailey   2. Peggy Conley   3. Laura Baugh
4. Belle Robertson   5. Jody Rosenthal   6. France
7. Spain   8. The Vagliano Trophy   9. Janet Melville
10. Pamela Barton

52 The Courses
1. Royal Dornoch   2. Pebble Beach, California (seventh hole)   3. Royal Birkdale (sixteenth green, 1961 Open)
4. Hoylake   5. La Moye   6. St George's, Sandwich (fourteenth hole)   7. The West Course at Wentworth
8. St Andrews (tenth hole)   9. Turnberry   10. Royal Lytham and St Annes

53 The European PGA Tour – the Europeans
1. The Dutch Open   2. Jose-Maria Canizares
3. Baldovino Dassu   4. Manuel Pinero   5. Manuel Ballesteros   6. Antonio Garrido   7. The Benson and Hedges International at Fulford, York   8. Bernhard Langer   9. Jose-Maria Olazabal   10. Jose Rivero

54 Mixed Bag
1. Sam Snead, 1946   2. Gary and Wayne Player   3. Ben Hogan   4. Doug Sanders   5. Eamonn Darcy   6. Francis Ouimet   7. Alexander 'Sandy' Herd   8. Gary Player
9. Lee Trevino   10. Jerry Pate

55 The Ryder Cup – Seasoned Competitors
1. Neil Coles   2. Christy O'Connor Snr   3. Dai Rees
4. Billy Casper   5. Arnold Palmer   6. Raymond Floyd
7. Sam Snead   8. Brian Huggett   9. Walter Hagen
10. Gene Sarazen

56 The US Masters – Low Scoring
1. Nick Price (South Africa)   2. Curtis Strange
3. Raymond Floyd   4. Johnny Miller   5. Ken Venturi
6. Art Wall   7. Lloyd Mangrum   8. Jack Nicklaus
9. Ben Hogan   10. Gary Player

57 The Open Championship – Outstanding Amateur Performances
1. Jose-Maria Olazabal   2. Hal Sutton   3. Peter McAvoy
4. Michael Bonallack   5. Ronnie Shade   6. Joe Carr
7. Reid Jack   8. Guy Wolstenholme   9. Willie Smith

10. Frank Stranahan

58 *The European WPGA Tour*
1. Kitrina Douglas   2. Ayako Okamoto   3. Kathy Whitworth   4. Dale Reid   5. Laurs Davies   6. Gillian Stewart   7. Jenny Lee Smith   8. Vanessa Marvin 9. Kitrina Douglas   10. Liselotte Nevmann

59 *Men's Amateur Golf – Britain in The Walker Cup*
1. Colin Montgomerie   2. Andrew Oldcorn   3. Ronan Rafferty   4. Peter Baker   5. Michael Bonallack 6. George MacGregor   7. St Andrews, 1983 and 1971 8. Joe Carr   9. John Beck   10. Rex and Lister Hartley

60 *The European PGA Tour – British Success*
1. Neil Coles   2. Nick Faldo   3. Tony Jacklin   4. Paul Way   5. Howard Clark   6. Warren Humphreys 7. Sandy Lyle   8. Robert Lee   9. Sam Torrance 10. Peter Butler

61 *The US Open Championship – Mixed Bag*
1. Jerry Pate   2. Hale Irwin   3. Tony Jacklin, 1970 4. Lee Trevino   5. Arnold Palmer   6. Ben Hogan 7. Julius Boros   8. Peter Thomson   9. Orville Moody 10. Jim Thorpe

62 *The US LPGA Tour*
1. Mildred 'Babe' Zaharias   2. Mickey Wright   3. Louise Suggs   4. Nancy Lopez   5. Hisako Higuchi   6. Betsy Rawls   7. Joanne Carner   8. Kathy Whitworth   9. The Vare Trophy (after Glenna Vare)   10. Patty Berg

63 *The US PGA Tour – Mixed Bag*
1. Hubert Green   2. Sam Snead   3. Jeff Mitchell   4. The Illinois Golf Classic at Oakwood Country Club, Illinois 5. Woody Blackburn   6. Donald 'D.A.' Weibring 7. Curtis Strange   8. Tom Watson   9. Mike Reid 10. Tom Watson

64 *The Open Championship – the First, the Last, the Only*
1. Bob Charles (NZ), Royal Lytham, 1963   2. Gary Player, 1959, 1968 and 1974   3. Sam Snead   4. Tom Watson, 1975   5. Richard Burton   6. Sandy Lyle, 1985 (aggregate 282, two over)   7. Arnaud Massy (France)

8. Walter Hagen   9. Bobby Jones   10. Peter Thomson, 1954–1956

65 *The US PGA Championship – Mixed Bag*
1. Don January   2. Bruce Crampton   3. Jim Ferrier
4. Gene Littler   5. Julius Boros   6. Sam Snead
7. Walter Burkemo   8. 1958   9. Lionel Hebert
10. Dow Finsterwald

66 *The Major Championships*
1. Tom Watson   2. Severiano Ballesteros   3. Jim Barnes
4. Larry Nelson, US Open 1983; US PGA 1987   5. Byron Nelson   6. Tom Watson, 1982   7. Jack Nicklaus
8. Bobby Jones, 1930   9. Tony Jacklin, 1969–1970
10. Gene Sarazen, US Open and PGA, 1922

67 *The Australasian Tour*
1. Bob Charles   2. Mark O'Meara   3. Bruce Devlin
4. Vaughan Somers   5. Wayne Smith   6. Gary Player
7. Greg Norman   8. Norman Von Nida   9. Sam
Torrance   10. Severiano Ballesteros

68 *Men's Amateur Golf – the Americans*
1. Jay Sigel   2. Nathaniel Crosby   3. Hal Sutton   4. Jack
Nicklaus   5. Gene Littler   6. Bill Hyndman   7. Bob
Dickson   8. Lawson Little   9. Frank Stranahan   10. Jess
Sweetser

69 *The European PGA Tour – Mixed Bag*
1. Dale Hayes   2. Billy Casper   3. Tony Jacklin   4. Jerry
Anderson   5. Bernhard Langer   6. Philip Parkin
7. Byron Nelson   8. Brian Huggett   9. David J. Russell
10. John O'Leary

70 *The Open Championship – Mixed Bag*
1. Gary Player   2. Hubert Green (USA)   3. Brian
Huggett   4. Hale Irwin   5. Bill Longmuir   6. The
Tooting Bec Cup   7. Henry Cotton, 1934, 1937 and
1948   8. Percy Alliss, father of Peter   9. Tom Morris Jnr,
1875   10. Bobby Locke (South Africa)

71 *The US Masters – Last-round Disasters*
1. Tom Kite   2. Ed Sneed   3. Charles Coody   4. Ken
Venturi   5. Jim Ferrier   6. Arnold Palmer   7. Hubert
Green   8. Ben Hogan   9. Ralph Guldahl   10. Greg
Norman

72 Ryder Cup – Mixed Bag
1. Tony Jacklin   2. Larry Nelson   3. Andy North
4. Eamonn Darcy   5. Muirfield, 1973   6. Lindrick, near
Sheffield   7. Arnold Palmer, 1963   8. Bernard and
Geoffrey Hunt   9. Percy and Peter Alliss   10. Jay and
Lionel Hebert

73 Mixed Bag
1. Roger Maltbie   2. Larry Mize   3. Scott Simpson
4. Lee Trevino   5. David Graham, 1979 US PGA, 1981
US Open   6. The Tunisian Open   7. Howard Clark
8. Lanny and Bobby Wadkins   9. Fred Haas   10. Walter
Hagen

74 The US PGA Tour – Winning Sequences
1. Bob Tway   2. Johnny Miller   3. Byron Nelson
4. Sam Snead   5. Gary Player   6. Billy Casper
7. Arnold Palmer   8. Jack Nicklaus   9. Ben Hogan
10. Jack Burke Jnr

75 The US Open Championship – Mixed Bag
1. John Mahaffey   2. Tom Watson   3. Forrest Fezler
4. Dave Hill   5. Jack Fleck   6. Ben Hogan, 1951
7. Merion, Pennsylvania   8. Ben Hogan   9. Lee Trevino
10. Isao Aoki (Japan)

76 The Open Championship – Mixed Bag
1. Kel Nagle   2. Harry Bradshaw   3. Gary Player
4. Johnny Miller   5. Henry Cotton, Sandwich, 1934
6. Fred Daly, 1947   7. Fred Bullock   8. Lu Liang Huan
(Mr Lu)   9. Lee Trevino   10. Masahiro Kuramoto

77 The European PGA Tour – the Commonwealth and South African Invasion
1. Greg Norman   2. Rodger Davis   3. Ian Baker-Finch
4. Mark McNulty   5. Graham Marsh   6. Wayne Grady
7. Rodger Davis   8. John Bland   9. Greg Turner
10. Jeff Hawkes

78 Ladies' Amateur Golf – Mixed Bag
1. Catherine Lacoste   2. Susan Shapcott   3. Marnie
McGuire (New Zealand)   4. May Hezlet   5. Julie Inkster
6. Glenna Collett (later Vare)   7. Kay Cockerill   8. Thion
de la Chaume, 1927, and Catherine Lacoste, 1969

9. Mildred (Didrikson) Zaharias   10. Joanne Carner (Gunderson)

79 *The World Matchplay Championship*
1. Tony Lema   2. Hale Irwin, 1974   3. Jack Nicklaus
4. Bill Rogers   5. David Graham   6. Graham Marsh
7. Simon Owen   8. Bob Charles   9. Tony Jacklin and Lee Trevino   10. Jack Nicklaus

80 *The Open Championship – Consistent Performers*
1. Roberto De Vicenzo (Argentina)   2. Jack Nicklaus, 1964 to 1979   3. Dai Rees   4. Peter Thomson
5. Arnold Palmer   6. Fred Daly   7. Flory Van Donck
8. Sam King   9. Alf Padgham   10. Kel Nagle

81 *The US PGA Tour – Young and First-time Winners*
1. Scott Verplank   2. Kenny Knox   3. Hal Sutton
4. Ben Crenshaw   5. Raymond Floyd   6. Arnold Palmer   7. Gene Littler   8. Calvin Peete   9. Joey Sindelar   10. Mike Hulbert

82 *The European PGA Tour – Mixed Bag*
1. Nick Faldo   2. Manuel Pinero   3. Neil Coles
4. Michael King   5. Isao Aoki   6. Norman Von Nida
7. Ramon Sota   8. Nick Faldo   9. Bernhard Langer
10. Ian Mosey

83 *Men's Amateur Golf – Mixed Bag*
1. Philippe Ploujoux   2. Jose-Maria Olazabal   3. Neville Sundelson   4. Richard Kaplan   5. Sam McCready
6. Peter Baker and Roger Roper   7. Jerry Haas, brother of Jay   8. Joe and Roddy Carr   9. Paul Downes   10. Brian Montgomery

84 *The Dunhill Nations Cup*
1. October 1985   2. The Old Course, St Andrews   3. Wales   4. Argentina   5. Japan   6. Australia   7. Greg Norman   8. England   9. Gordon J. Brand (England)
10. Curtis Strange

85 *The US Senior Tour*
1. Bruce Crampton   2. Peter Thomson   3. Dale Douglas
4. Gary Player   5. Juan 'Chi Chi' Rodriguez   6. Miller Barber   7. Guy Wolstenholme   8. Roberto de Vicenzo
9. Rod Funseth   10. Bob Charles

86 *The World Cup*
1. Flory Van Donck (Belgium)   2. Angel and Sebastian Miguel   3. Harry Bradshaw and Christy O'Connor
4. Jimmy Demaret   5. Wentworth   6. Bernard Hunt and Harry Weetman   7. Taiwan   8. Kel Nagle   9. Bruce Devlin and David Graham   10. Greg Norman

87 *The Open Championship – the First, the Last, the Only*
1. Jack Nicklaus   2. Tom Watson, 1977, 268 strokes
3. Tommy Armour   4. Bobby Jones, 1926   5. Henry Cotton   6. Willie Park   7. Jim Barnes   8. Mark Hayes (USA)   9. Greg Norman, 1986   10. Tom Kidd

88 *The European PGA Tour – the Americans*
1. Craig Stadler   2. Lee Trevino   3. Tom Kite   4. Gay Brewer   5. Charles Coody   6. Arnold Palmer   7. Bobby Wadkins   8. The Lancôme Trophy   9. Ben Crenshaw
10. Bob Byman

89 *The Major Championships*
1. Greg Norman   2. Lee Trevino   3. Ben Crenshaw
4. Gary Player   5. Harry Vardon   6. Bobby Jones, 1926
7. Tommy Armour   8. Walter Hagen   9. Sam Snead
10. Tom Weiskopf

90 *The South African Tour*
1. Gary Player   2. David Frost   3. Bobby Cole   4. Denis Watson   5. Mark McNulty   6. Vincent Tshabalala
7. Sid Brews   8. Lee Trevino   9. Tom Weiskopf
10. Harold Henning

91 *The US PGA Tour – Overseas Winners*
1. Greg Norman   2. Gary Player   3. Bobby Locke
4. Graham Marsh   5. Nick Price   6. Denis Watson
7. Bruce Crampton   8. Bernhard Langer   9. Severiano Ballesteros   10. Bob Charles

92 *Men's Amateur Golf – Expert Mixed Bag*
1. Harold Hilton   2. Lawson Little, 1934 and 1935
3. Australia   4. Jack Nicklaus   5. Japan   6. Walter J. Travis   7. Hal Sutton and Bob Tway   8. Sweden
9. Eleven   10. The World Amateur Team Championship

93 *The Open Championship – Expert Mixed Bag*
1. Harold Hilton   2. Roger Wethered   3. Gene Sarazen
4. Jose Jurado, who came second with a round of 77

5. Arthur Havers   6. Jack White, 296   7. Maurice Flitcroft   8. Craig Wood   9. Musselburgh   10. Harry Vardon, 1896 and 1911

94 *The US Open Championship – Expert Mixed Bag*
1. Ken Venturi   2. Sam Snead   3. Johnny Goodman
4. Bobby Jones, 1922–1930   5. Billy Burke   6. Tommy Bolt
7. Jim Barnes   8. John McDermott   9. Ben Hogan
10. Ralph Guldahl

95 *The US Masters – Expert Mixed Bag*
1. Tom Weiskopf   2. Charles Coody   3. Arnold Palmer
4. Jack Burke Jnr   5. Jimmy Demaret   6. Ralph Guldahl
7. Ben Hogan.   8. Billy Casper   9. Johnny Miller
10. Miller Barber

96 *The US PGA Championship – Expert Mixed Bag*
1. Walter Hagen   2. Ben Hogan   3. Lionel Hebert, 1957 and Jay Hebert, 1960   4. Ellsworth Vine   5. Jim Barnes
6. Paul Runyan   7. Gene Sarazen   8. Byron Nelson
9. Dane Marr   10. Doug Sanders

97 *The US Open Championship – Expert Low Scoring*
1. Tom Weiskopf   2. Ben Crenshaw   3. Tony Manero
4. Bert Yancey   5. Gene Borek   6. Ray McBee   7. Gene Sarazen   8. Tommy Jacobs   9. Jack Nicklaus   10. Gene Sarazen

98 *The US Masters – Expert Mixed Bag*
1. Frank Stranahan   2. Billy Joe Patton   3. Charles Coe
4. Ramon Sota   5. Craig Wood   6. Jack Nicklaus
7. Horton Smith   8. Gene Sarazen   9. Fuzzy Zoeller
10. Craig Wood

99 *The Open Championship – Expert Mixed Bag*
1. The Challenge Belt   2. Peter Thomson, 1954 and 1965   3. John Henry Taylor   4. George Duncan
5. Sandy Herd   6. James Braid   7. Royal St Georges, Sandwich (1894)   8. Whitcombe (Reg: first in 1938, second in 1937, third in 1939; Ernest: second in 1924; Charles: third in 1935)   9. John Ball   10. Sid Brews

100 *The US Open Championship – Expert Mixed Bag*
1. Harry Vardon and Ted Ray   2. Francis Ouimet
3. Jerome Travers   4. Alex Smith   5. Horace Rawlins

6. Willie Smith 7. Walter Hagen 8. Bobby Jones, 1923–1929 9. Willie Anderson 10. Charles 'Chick' Evans

101 *1988 Open Championship*
1. Severiano Ballesteros 2. Nick Price (70, 67, 69, 69)
3. Sandy Lyle 4. Paul Broadhurst 5. Lanny Wadkins
6. David J. Russell 7. Bob Charles 8. Craig Stradler
9. Fred Couples and Gary Koch 10. Brad Faxon

102 *1988 US Masters and US Open Championships*
1. Sandy Lyle 2. Mark Calcavecchia 3. Greg Norman
4. Ian Woosnam 5. Curtis Strange 6. Jack Nicklaus
7. Bill Mayfair (USA) 8. Scott Simpson 9. Peter Jacobsen 10. Curtis Strange

103 *1988 European Tour*
1. David Whelan 2. David Llewellyn 3. Severiano Ballesteros (in addition, he was disqualified from the 1983 Silk Cut Masters for signing his card for the wrong score)
4. Derrick Cooper 5. Bernhard Langer 6. Richard Boxall 7. Sandy Lyle 8. Jose-Maria Olazabal 9. Denis Durnian 10. Barry Lane

104 *Mixed Bag – 1988*
1. Guy Wuollett 2. David Feherty 3. Steve Pate
4. Christian Hardin 5. Chris Platts (son of Lionel)
6. Fred Couples 7. Claire Hourihane 8. Chip Beck
9. Vijay Singh 10. Ken Green

THE MENSA
PUZZLE · BOOK

PHILIP CARTER & KEN RUSSELL

This challenging collection of Mensa puzzles is not for the faint-hearted. You'll need all your wits about you to solve the dazzling range of brainteasers – crosswords, word and number games, grid and diagram puzzles – a veritable cornucopia of craftiness.

THE ULTIMATE QUIZ BOOK FOR THE ULTIMATE QUIZ ADDICT

0 7474 0018 7   CROSSWORDS/QUIZZES   £2.99

_T_RACKDOWN _1_

HUNT FOR HIDDEN KNOWLEDGE!

You'll need stealth and guile, ingenuity and
inventiveness to solve these unputdownable
puzzles! Combining the absorption of a word
search puzzle with the added stimulus of
uncovering a fascinating fact, TRACKDOWN
is an irresistible cocktail of cunning
craftiness!

0 7474 0008 3   CROSSWORDS/QUIZZES   £1.99

And don't miss:
TRACKDOWN VOLUME 2
also available in Sphere Books

FICTION

JUBILEE: THE POPPY CHRONICLES 1	Claire Rayner	£3.50 ☐
DAUGHTERS	Suzanne Goodwin	£3.50 ☐
REDCOAT	Bernard Cornwell	£3.50 ☐
WHEN DREAMS COME TRUE	Emma Blair	£3.50 ☐
THE LEGACY OF HEOROT	Niven/Pournelle/Barnes	£3.50 ☐

FILM AND TV TIE-IN

BUSTER	Colin Shindler	£2.99 ☐
COMING TOGETHER	Alexandra Hine	£2.99 ☐
RUN FOR YOUR LIFE	Stuart Collins	£2.99 ☐
BLACK FOREST CLINIC	Peter Heim	£2.99 ☐
INTIMATE CONTACT	Jacqueline Osborne	£2.50 ☐

NON-FICTION

BARE-FACED MESSIAH	Russell Miller	£3.99 ☐
THE COCHIN CONNECTION	Alison and Brian Milgate	£3.50 ☐
HOWARD & MASCHLER ON FOOD	Elizabeth Jane Howard and Fay Maschler	£3.99 ☐
FISH	Robyn Wilson	£2.50 ☐
THE SACRED VIRGIN AND THE HOLY WHORE	Anthony Harris	£3.50 ☐

All Sphere books are available at your local bookshop or newsagent, or can be ordered direct from the publisher. Just tick the titles you want and fill in the form below.

Name_____

Address_____

_____

Write to Sphere Books, Cash Sales Department, P.O. Box 11, Falmouth, Cornwall TR10 9EN

Please enclose a cheque or postal order to the value of the cover price plus:

UK: 60p for the first book, 25p for the second book and 15p for each additional book ordered to a maximum charge of £1.90.

OVERSEAS & EIRE: £1.25 for the first book, 75p for the second book and 28p for each subsequent title ordered.

BFPO: 60p for the first book, 25p for the second book plus 15p per copy for the next 7 books, thereafter 9p per book.

Sphere Books reserve the right to show new retail prices on covers which may differ from those previously advertised in the text elsewhere, and to increase postal rates in accordance with the P.O.